C000259042

THE ULTIMATE GUIDE TO DRIVER TRAINING

BILL LAVENDER

mydriving.co.uk
driven to drive better

My Driving Ltd, 16 Station Parade. The Broadway, Elm Park, Hornchurch, RM12 5AB.

ISBN: 978-1-3999-2466-5

First Published as How to become a Driving Instructor 2013.

The information provided in this Guide is accurate at the time of publication. Legislation, regulations, and statistics are subject to change with the passage of time. To stay up to date, subscribe to the DVSA's email list and join one or more of the national trainer associations listed in the Network Contacts appendix at the back of this guide. Through them you can find out about local ADI groups.

Our free document library provides learning resources, including full lesson plans, colour diagrams along with a summary update of the most recent changes to the Highway Code, available as a hard copy since April 2022. We say a very special thank you to the ADINJC for their kind permission to allow us to publish this excellent summary. This is a "must read" for every driver trainer at: https://mydriving.co.uk/wp-content/uploads/2022/04/Highway-Code-changes-2022.pdf

www.mydriving.co.uk

Formed in 1996 by Bill Lavender, the original focus was online resources. "Driving Online" was one of the first UK driving websites.

The site remains independent and still retains its identity as an information resource, particularly for driver trainers and their learners. The most popular downloads are our lesson plans and colour versions of all the diagrams included in this guide.

In April 2021, "MyDriving" re-launched as a driving school, predominantly operating in East London. Our experience in the driving school industry makes us unique. Our vision is to teach learners in a relaxed and enjoyable way, using the "Goals for Driver Education". We are convinced that this is **the** way to stay collision-free after passing the driving test.

From the website, users can find an easy link to our Facebook pages. We use these to link to issues or items of interest for learners, drivers, and driver trainers. It is also easy to have a chat if you have any questions or queries.

mydriving.co.uk
driven to drive better

FOREWORD
By Paul Caddick
Editor, Intelligent Instructor

Becoming an Approved Driving Instructor (ADI) is a fantastic career choice. You will be providing an essential service to society, learning professional teaching skills that give individuals autonomy and help them to realise their dreams. Meanwhile, you can earn a good income, in a flexible and self-determined business, whilst positively contributing to saving lives and reducing the unnecessary carnage on the roads. As a driver trainer, you make a huge difference to the improvement of road safety. That is something to truly be proud of, and it's an occupation that deserves genuine respect.

However, becoming a driver trainer is not just about sitting in the passenger seat and giving instructions to nervous teenagers behind the wheel. The work and the people you teach are as varied as anything you can imagine. This is what makes it both an exciting and fulfilling area of work, as well as challenging and demanding.

So, to make a success of this, you need to understand the subject matter, learn effective teaching skills, and be open to seeing and accepting new perspectives. These are just a few of the reasons why becoming a driver trainer is such a rewarding experience—the wheels of the world never stop turning, and you never stop learning.

As you start out on this journey, there is no better co-pilot to have in the passenger seat than Bill Lavender. He has decades of experience in driver training, first qualifying as an ADI in 1982. He worked his way up the ladder with the original driving school, BSM (British School of Motoring). From teaching new drivers, he became responsible for developing the company's learning resources and helping train new ADIs. He set up National Vocational Qualifications (NVQ) and BTEC awards within the BSM business before going on to run his own driver training business, driving school, and consultancy service. Now working in the training of emergency response drivers, principally with the ambulance service, he also specialises in Continuing Professional Development for ADIs, along with Driver Certificate of Professional Competence (DCPC) for professional bus and lorry drivers.

It is difficult to think of any areas in this industry that Bill has not experienced, been involved in, or left his stamp on. I first came across his wealth of abilities, skills, and knowledge when setting up and managing *adiNEWS* magazine. Bill's understanding and experience was a brilliant addition to the publication, and he soon became established as a very respected, regular contributor to what was the number one magazine for the industry. When I later founded the award-winning *Intelligent Instructor* magazine, Bill was the first person I contacted to be a contributor, such was his popularity and importance to the readership.

In this book, Bill provides a clear and unique guide to becoming a driver trainer. Utilising his extensive knowledge, hands-on experience, and effective writing skills, he provides you with a clear path to training success, ongoing achievements, and a rewarding career in driver training.

If you want to become a good ADI, this is the book for you. Bill's deep understanding and wide experience of the industry, along with his informative and honest writing style, makes him the perfect authority on how to become a great driver trainer. Using Bill's insider strategies, I have no doubt that you will succeed.

Paul Caddick
January 2023

INTRODUCTION
By Bill Lavender
How to Become a Driver Trainer

Teaching people to drive is an essential service to society. Without drivers, what would our world be like? How would food and products get to shops and stores, and how would deliveries be made? Driving is a fundamental part of modern life, whether it involves commuting, travelling, or visiting family and friends; and that's not forgetting the emergency services, which use driven vehicles to rescue patients.

So, we've established that nearly every aspect of modern life requires drivers, but to become a driver you need to be **taught** the mechanics of operating the vehicle, as well as the correct understanding of using the vehicle on the road in a safe, responsible, and proper manner. Without the skill and dedication of driver trainers, the modern world would quickly grind to a chaotic, juddering standstill.

Since you've purchased a copy of this book, it looks like you are deciding whether to embark on providing a key professional service to your community and your country, bringing with it both respect and responsibilities. I can tell you that being a driver trainer is an exciting and fun career that sees you out and about, meeting people of all ages and all backgrounds. Whilst being a highly satisfying and rewarding job, it also provides the opportunity to be your own boss and work flexible hours that suit you and your needs, whilst earning a good living. This is a career that allows you to make a real and positive difference to your own and other people's lives.

In truth, "driver trainer" is a more accurate label for the work of those who teach and develop driving skills. Becoming **qualified** is much more than starting a new job; it is about learning the skills of a whole new profession: the art of teaching. While the official DVSA (Driver Vehicle Standards Agency) qualification remains ADI (Approved Driving Instructor), the industry and the job has evolved. Now, it's widely recognised that teaching people to drive is less about basic instruction techniques and more about coaching.

Britain's roads are some of the safest, not only in Europe, but in the world. It is very satisfying to consider that the skills you are teaching will provide a foundation for good driving and make a valuable contribution to road safety. This job is about more than just your students — it is about giving something positive to everyone. That's because the main responsibility of ADIs is help people learn to drive safely on the road, as well as successfully preparing them for their driving tests. This involves monitoring the road and other vehicles very carefully, as well as watching the learner, and being prepared to simultaneously give instruction or coach the learner through traffic situations.

Learner drivers do not make deliberate mistakes. However, they are likely to make fewer errors where the trainer is proactive and in control of the learning environment, giving the correct level of tuition. To achieve this, a good trainer will use and adapt their teaching methods according to the needs of the student and the situation, always applying best practice.

Besides an interest in driving, the starting point is having an even temperament and a friendly and helpful personality. Some trainers find it easier than others to be understanding, supportive, and capable of developing a good rapport with customers. Each learner driver has a different character and personality. You need to be patient and open to their needs—it is not always easy to be the "perfect driver". When spending your time sitting next to people who cannot drive, there is a tremendous amount of satisfaction seeing them develop into great drivers under your tutelage.

It can be a long road to qualifying as an ADI, taking at least a year from making the application. Studying and preparing yourself for each part of the qualifying examination is likely to take up much of your time, and will undoubtedly involve the support of people who are close to you.

DRIVING FORWARD TO SUCCESS

You only get one opportunity to make a good first impression. So, always begin with a smile. You are your best advertisement, so make sure that you look the part. This doesn't mean you need to wear a suit; you can dress in comfortable clothing but take care to look smart. Keep your car in a clean and roadworthy condition, always driving in a professional manner.

During lessons, the learner's concentration can easily fade, even after less than ten minutes. A good trainer will need to recognise this and find ways to stimulate the learner. This could involve pulling over to review, before continuing with the drive. The ultimate skill for an effective trainer is excellent verbal communication. Most of the time your classroom is moving on four wheels, so consider the force, pitch and quality of your voice, and the timing or speed of speaking. Make sure that you have no distracting mannerisms and use humour only if it is relevant. It goes without saying that sexism, racism, and homophobia are unacceptable. Also, avoid stereotyping other road users, for instance, drivers of more powerful cars or other types of vehicles.

Adapting non-verbal communication is a very important skill. Most experts agree that 70% to 93% of all communication is non-verbal. Non-verbal communication is a two-way interaction between learner and trainer where, for instance, various hand or arm gestures, head movements, facial expressions, and eye contact will indicate feelings such as approval or disapproval, understanding, willingness, satisfaction, a desire to interrupt, frustration, or defensiveness.

Most experienced driver trainers would say that you need to be a "people person" to succeed in this line of work. They would also say that they enjoy driving and aspire to achieve a high first-time pass rate. However, as trainers' personalities and characters differ, so do their approaches to the job. A serious challenge facing all professional driver trainers is that driving is regarded as a common and easy activity. But for nearly everyone, it is the most dangerous thing they will ever do in their lives. Traffic collisions are the most common cause of death and serious injury in the world, with young people being particularly vulnerable. This is why driver trainers are so important and so valued: the one-to-one situation, usually for forty hours or more, puts the driver trainer in a powerful position to influence the behaviour of the next generation of drivers. Once qualified, drivers, by default, are often very defensive about their driving skills and dislike criticism, so it is easier to modify the attitudes of provisional licence holders.

Hopefully you understand now that being a good driver trainer is about more than just teaching people how to pass their driving test. As a driver trainer, you are at the forefront of road safety, and can make a real impact in reducing traffic collision figures. You are a lifesaver, a game-changer, and a pioneer for driver safety and awareness.

This is an exciting, indeed revolutionary time to join this industry. Why? Because electric vehicles are becoming more common place on our roads. Instead of lessons on operating a manual gearbox, learners need only learn to drive a vehicle with automatic transmission. The change to electric vehicles brings about some differences in our teaching content, such as regenerative braking – a different feel for the accelerator; no gears or clutch, even driving with one pedal, conserving battery power, how to charge an EV etc, etc.

If you decide that becoming a driver trainer is for you, it is our hope that the guidance in this book will help provide the framework and skills to perform the job to the highest standards and ensure you achieve professional career success. I have the utmost confidence that this book can help you to do just that. So, let's get started!

Bill Lavender.

Bill Lavender BA (Hons) Cert Ed /
Award for Services to Road Safety
January 2023

CONTENTS

CHAPTER 1

WHY BECOME A DRIVER TRAINER?

Is this a job I can do?

This is a hugely important question: why indeed would anyone seriously contemplate becoming a driver trainer?

When answering this question, a well-known Bob Newhart comedy sketch from the 1970s comes to mind. During this, the American comedian depicts a series of difficult situations occurring during a driving lesson. While Bob struggles extremely hard to keep a grip of the lesson, his customer still enjoys it and asks to book more training! If you have not seen the sketch, you can easily find it on the internet using YouTube.

WHAT ARE THE ROLES AND RESPONSIBILITIES?

The formal responsibilities almost speak for themselves in terms of teaching "safe driving for life". As an ambassador of the road, you are relied upon to set a good example in your own driving, and ensure that pupils are kept in a safe learning environment whilst they gain experience behind the wheel. The roles that come into focus while teaching someone to drive can be quite varied. Besides being a teacher or a coach, when giving advice you are an advisor; when drawing diagrams you are an artist, and when listening you might even say that you are a counsellor or a psychologist.

THE UK DRIVER

Most people in Britain will have taken a full course of professional driving lessons when learning to drive. Some of us will have had the advantage of private practise between lessons as well. So, we have an idea of what the work entails and what is involved. No doubt we also all have opinions on driving standards and views on how these should be improved. Each of us will probably have at least one interesting or amusing story to tell about something that happened during our training, or perhaps an incident during the driving test itself. Driving is an easy and popular topic for discussion; everyone knows best, even though over three million out of a total 32 million drivers here in the UK have penalty points on their licences. This does not stop us from being expert advisors, even those who don't drive!

CAREER CHOICE?

You must be at least 21 and have held a full car licence for at least four years before you can qualify with the Driver and Vehicle Standards Agency (DVSA) as an Approved Driver Instructor (ADI). This could be one reason why the career is not promoted to school leavers. If you want to be a bus or lorry driver trainer then there is less regulation. All that you will need is to have held that class of driving licence for at least three years, and then you can find a company to employ you (unless you already have your own training vehicle).

ADIs are drawn from a very wide range of different backgrounds, representing just about every industry, business, and profession that you can think of. For some people, the profession can form a second income. The most common denominator is an interest in driving cars. Though the national television advertisements—which promised high income and attracted redundant and unemployed workers—disappeared from our TV screens some years ago, the career still has a vocational appeal for those who enjoy motoring and feel that they can do a good job teaching people.

WHAT ARE THE ATTRACTIONS?

Most full-time driver trainers are self-employed. Being your own boss means not having to report to someone else, which can be a great feeling. You still need to be good with your time management; to keep your customers you will need to be reliable and punctual. In the long run, it might also be an opportunity to improve your work/life balance. The career might be something you wish to pursue on a part-time basis, possibly while keeping your day job.

Although it is an advantage to manage the times that you want to work, there can be some disadvantages, such as needing to work in the evenings or at weekends. You will need to find or make time to manage your financial accounts and arrange your own tax payments. If you are unsure of how to do this, it is a sensible option to engage the services of a professional accountant.

CHAPTER 2

WHAT IS THE WORK LIKE?

What's involved?

For the right person, the work is extremely rewarding. However, if you consider yourself to be a perfect driver and enjoy driving; sitting next to people who are learning to drive can be challenging!

All areas of the driver training industry have for many years referred to the DVSA's driving test marking form, the DL25, as a basis for training and development. Since 2012 the industry has been encouraged to adapt to the "National Standards" for driving cars and vans. These are produced in an NVQ format and are available for download online, giving guidance to both trainers and new drivers covering competencies and the performance outcomes that the DVSA is expecting.

With each new learner, the training format remains the same. Trainers check about any previous driving or other relevant experience, such as riding a pedal cycle or perhaps a motorbike. If the learner has driven a car before, we begin by making a practical assessment of what skills and knowledge they have. Based on the result of this, then we can plan a series of lessons up to the point where they are ready to take their practical driving test. Trainers are encouraged to link practical training with the theory and hazard perception elements. Most trainers seem content for learners to study independently, in their own time, often using a phone app. A lot of learners fail the multiple-choice element because of their weak knowledge of the Highway Code.

Most driving lessons follow a similar pattern, typically covering these areas:

1. **Eyesight, licence, insurance, basic vehicle and pre-driving checks**. Driving licences must be valid for the category of vehicle being driven and adequate insurance cover needs to be in place. Drivers have a responsibility to comply with "Construction and Use Regulations", therefore regular checks need to include bodywork, windows, and wiper blades. Daily vehicle checks will include fuel, engine fluid levels such as oil and coolant, lights, and tyre pressures. Before moving off, each driver needs to complete a cockpit drill.

2. **Car controls, equipment, and components**. Begin with the functions and use of the accelerator, footbrake, clutch, gears, steering, and handbrake. Detail the auxiliary controls and the dual controls. Also

include the benefits of ABS and electronic stability programmes; safe use of satellite navigation, dash-cam and any other fitted in-car technologies. Use of Personal Protective Equipment (PPE) such as high visibility clothing may be a requirement when delivering lessons on corporate contracts.

3. **Vehicle characteristics**. Examples include knowing the principles concerning use of speed and braking distances. This should also include vehicle road holding under various road and weather conditions.

4. **Road Procedure**. Examples include the knowledge and skills to carry out the observation routine recommended in the 'Highway Code':
Mirrors – Signal – Manoeuvre (MSM).

5. **Road user behaviour**. Examples include knowledge of the most common causes of collisions, which road users are most at risk, and how to reduce that risk.

6. **Adapting to different driving and traffic conditions**. Examples include knowing the hazards in both daylight and darkness, and when using different types of road.

7. **Motoring law and the "Highway Code"**. Examples include personal fitness to drive—alcohol, drugs, fatigue, stress, and illness; sufficient knowledge about traffic signs, road markings, pedestrian crossing types and parking regulations; accident reporting procedures.

8. **Environmental Issues**. For example, a responsible driving technique will minimise the impact on the environment, as well as achieving fuel cost savings and reducing wear and tear on the vehicle.

9. **Dealing with emergency situations**. It is important that new drivers know the actions needed to avoid and correct skids, how to drive through floods and flooded areas, and what to do when involved in a collision or breakdown. They also must know the correct driving procedures when emergency vehicles are approaching with a blue light on.

10. **Attitude**. Develop a positive attitude to all other drivers and road users. Most driver mistakes, although annoying, are made unintentionally and need to be tolerated. Say to yourself: 'Let it go'. This is an element of the "Goals for Driver Education" (GDE Matrix)—an internationally agreed framework for structuring driver coaching and progress.

For the safety of learners, yourself, and other road users, you will normally teach in a manual car fitted with dual brake and clutch pedals (dual controls). As the learner becomes more competent, you will leave the "nursery patch" and take them to busier roads, dual carriageways, and more complex junctions, including roundabouts. Once you believe the learner has reached a high enough standard, you can advise them on applying for a driving test date. To help judge this date, it is useful to conduct a mock driving test that simulates the real thing. You might wish to choose an associate ADI to conduct this for you.

Electric cars are rapidly increasing in popularity. With the end of the traditional internal combustion engine, learners will no longer need to learn how to change gears and use the clutch. All electric vehicles are automatic. They are much easier, safer and better to drive.

WHAT SKILLS OR QUALIFICATIONS ARE NEEDED?

No formal academic qualifications are needed in. However, before you can qualify as a Driving and Vehicle Standards Agency (DVSA) Approved Driving Instructor (ADI), you need to be at least 21 years old and have held a driving licence for over three years. You should not have any motoring convictions and will have to pass an enhanced "Disclosure and Barring Service (DBS) Check". The ADI examination process is in three parts, that need to be completed within two years.

Unless you are already a qualified teacher and advanced driver, you are unlikely to pass the qualifying examination without taking an appropriate training course. This may be with a large national driving instructor training provider, or perhaps an approved local individual trainer.

DRIVING TEST "KNOW-HOW"

Learners will expect you to have an insight into how the driving test is conducted and assessed, so give them advice accordingly. The DVSA have in recent years actively encouraged ADIs to sit-in and watch driving tests being conducted on their students. The number of trainers doing so has risen from around 5% to over 20%. Observing driving tests is the best way to see the standard that students must meet in order to pass the test, and to drive unaccompanied. Of course, it is important to discuss with your learner about accompanying them on their test. It is their choice, and they may prefer that you do not sit in.

During the practical test, the examiner will assess and record any errors. The driving test report form, known as the DL25, is completed electronically using an iPad. The system of negative marking that is used achieves a straightforward pass or fail result. Some things that we might, as trainers, consider to be mistakes or discussion issues, may be judged as "unworthy of note". The most common marking is a "driving fault", incorrectly referred to by many ADIs as a "minor fault". Saying that the fault is "only minor" suggests that it is unimportant, when in other circumstances things could be quite different. "Serious faults" are recorded where there was potential danger; or where driving faults are being repeated. The remaining category is a "dangerous fault", which may involve the need for evasive action by another road user, or some verbal or physical intervention by the examiner.

Once the level of faults has been assessed, this will be recorded electronically. At the end of the test, any accumulation of faults will have been calculated. A test fail will result, where a candidate has 16 or more driving faults; or one or more serious or dangerous faults.

Unlike lessons, the format of the driving test prevents the examiner addressing rooted behavioural or psychological factors. Nonetheless, by observing driving tests, a great level of technical "know-how" can be learnt very quickly and efficiently. Other practical "know-how" is the management of test bookings, including the preferred test centre location. This will help avoid appointment clashes or having too many tests in the same business week. As part of the training programme, trainers need to manage these arrangements. This administration work can easily be performed online using the DVSA booking facility for customers.

Because of increasing traffic and changes to the driving test, the amount of time needed to learn the essentials is taking longer. However, students and parents often expect the training period to be shorter, so it is important to manage expectations. There are no real shortcuts to first-time driving test success; what counts the most is quality time spent training and practising behind the wheel. A natural follow-on from a successful driving test result is to take the "Pass Plus" course.

The government introduced this voluntary training scheme in 1995. The idea is that newly-qualified drivers take further training, with the aim being to improve road safety and help reduce the risk of costly collisions. The scheme consolidates and builds on previous learning. If you promote and sell this concept during basic training, it will not only benefit the new driver but will help improve your business earnings too.

Finally, as in every job, there are important elements of paperwork to complete. You will need to keep an up-to-date appointment diary for customers, along with a record of your business income and expenditure for taxation purposes. Keep all your payment receipts and perhaps set up a separate business bank account. There are companies advertised that provide various levels of administrative help, diary management, and accountancy services that can save you time and stress, helping to ensure an efficient, automated, and professional business structure.

CHAPTER 3

CUSTOMER CARE

Meeting client expectations

You have had the enquiry, with the usual questions: How much are your lessons? What are your discounts? How many lessons will I need to pass?

You discuss your services with the prospective customer, or the person(s) paying for their lessons. You sell the benefits and advantages of the way you teach people to drive, and you make the sale. Your new customer has a provisional driving licence, and is very keen and ready to begin practical driving lessons...

So, now what?

SECRET IS IN THE PREPARATION

First impressions are the most lasting. With this in mind, it is particularly important to get things right. Is your car ready? Are you looking your best, dressed professionally? What are the ground rules for the course of lessons, what you expect from students, and what they can expect from you? How will you plan and manage their training course?

- If the first lesson was booked with a phone call, will this be their normal means of contact?

- Where is the pick-up point: home, work, or somewhere else?

- When and how will you present your business terms and conditions?

- Do you expect lesson payment before starting?

- Will you always keep one lesson payment in credit, to discourage cancellations?

- Do you know what your new customer's needs are? Is the person a complete beginner or at some other stage in the learning process?

- Do they have any medical issues, learning difficulties, or special needs?

- Have you checked their eyesight and driving licence?

THINK PROFESSIONAL

We need to know our customers as individuals. Likewise, we need to understand the impression that we will have on them. Without a regular stream of new customers, whether sourced through recommendations or other means, you will not have a business. As mentioned previously, **you** are your best advert, so you need to be promoting the best of you all the time. The trappings do, therefore, matter; we should consider things like our grooming, clothes, and our tone of voice. We should be open and friendly but also exude confidence, without appearing arrogant or overbearing. We should also mind our manners by avoiding sexual innuendo, sarcasm, offensive comments, or jokes that are in bad taste. We need to be respected, valued, and even liked so that we can deliver our teaching more effectively, but also gain more business through the recommendations and testimonials of our students/customers.

INFLUENCES

When customers are asked about what they want from learning to drive, they are likely to say, 'I want to pass my driving test.' Becoming a full licence holder means independence from rigid public transport and costly taxis. Driving means having the freedom to get around much more easily, going where you want, when you want. While there has been some tendency to demonise driving and cars as something politically incorrect, in the real world having a driving licence significantly improves job and career prospects.

The influence of peers can be a factor affecting the decisions students make, such as choice of trainer or the training car they wish to learn in. Their parents, who may have agreed to fund some or all their lessons, are inclined to understate both the amount of time they personally took learning to drive, as well as the cost. So, providing a positive reality check is important to avoid frustrations later on.

A good way to increase business leads without advertising, is to offer existing learners commercial incentives. For instance, you could suggest that for every new introduction you receive via them, they will receive a reduced-price lesson, or some other discount or commercial offer.

However, in reality, the best way to get good recommendations is to be great at what you do. Ensure that customers enjoy their lessons with you, and that learning has been achieved. If you combine this with your good attention and respect, ensuring they are always aware of where they are at in the learning process, celebrating their successes while setting realistic goals, then they will feel that they have received value for money. In this way, you can expect plenty of personal recommendations. This is the bedrock to establishing, developing, and keeping a flourishing business—not just in the driving industry but everywhere else too.

CHAPTER 4

HOW TO MAKE A LIVING

Can I make money?

The RAC has calculated that, including driving license and test fees, but without the cost of insurance for private practise, the average learner driver will spend £1,551 to become a fully qualified motorist. There are always learners looking for trainers: the question is whether you are able to find them yourself, or whether you need to join a local or national driving school to help.

WHAT IS THE MARKET?

The number of people turning 17 in 2020 was 695,549. From 2021-2025, this number looks set to increase significantly (due to population growth), and is projected to reach 795,000 people in 2025. Likewise, the COVID-19 pandemic of 2020/21 has seriously interrupted training and testing, leading to a large backlog of learners in the system. This will take some time to clear, and the DVSA have already set plans to increase the numbers of examiners available, as well as increasing driving test slots.

The pandemic has also seen a reduction in the number of driver trainers; a number have taken the opportunity to retire, and others had to find work in different areas whilst testing and training was suspended. Many of these people decided not to return to the industry. This is a good thing: it means that there are plenty of students looking for driving lessons, and demand for your services will be high.

In the year up to April 2020, almost 1.3 million people took a car driving test. The current practical test pass averages at 45%. This includes multiple attempts.

WHO ARE OUR COMPETITORS?

There are currently 38,842 Approved Driving Instructors (ADIs) on the DVSA Register. The number of ADIs continues to fall, following years of gradual rising. Many ADIs gained the qualification while they were between other jobs, or because they are/were involved in another professional area of road safety.

LESSON PRICES

You need to work out what all your business costs are, then fix your price. You can get help from one of the trade associations to work the figures out accurately. Remember that driving schools often advertise an initial lesson price discount to entice new customers. If you intend on working as an independent trainer, to ensure commercial viability, your business plan must assume that most lessons will be given at the full cost rate.

Not all trainers are experienced business thinkers. There is a belief that learners consider driving lessons to be expensive, and that they will shop around, taking advantage of each driving school's special "starting offer". In context, most things purchased in life can be considered expensive, such as sitting in a taxi or mini-cab for an hour's journey. Comparisons with other kinds of tutoring, such as with musical instruments and sports, suggest the level where the pricing for the "going-rate" for driving lessons needs to be. Are you charging what you are worth?

When it comes to driving lessons, price (as in all industries), is determined by the market. The best way to retain learners on a full-price lesson is to ensure a service difference. Remember that it may not be the learner who is making the buying decision; it might be parents who are paying for the training. But, whoever is paying, you will need to be able to prove a point of difference that they see as beneficial. In business, this is referred to as a Unique Selling Point (USP). Customer satisfaction and recommendations are the way forward to increase potential business earnings.

Trainers who attract learners with cheap lessons may well be the ones to have the worst reputation. Low-cost lessons can be associated with poor quality training and inevitable customer disappointment, such as repeated driving test failures. It is normal to have a separate charge for the use of your training vehicle for the driving test. This should be calculated on a minimum of an hour's use driving to the test centre; the duration of the test, and return to an agreed destination. Some learners might wrongly assume that this hire fee is included in the DVSA test fee. There is a significant safety risk associated with learners who contact you to hire your car for only the test, and you should be prepared to refuse use of the vehicle if their driving standard is unsafe.

HOW MUCH DO DRIVER TRAINERS EARN?

In terms of income expectations, establishing a new business will always take some time, and its growth will depend on good planning and a full commitment. Some experienced trainers can turn over £40,000 a year. However, this is an optimistic assumption, and it cannot be taken as an average. Typical income must be based on the cost of an hourly driving lesson and the amount of hours worked. Lessons fees range on average from around £25 to around £40 an hour, and some trainers may be prepared to work more than 48 hours a week. Costs (car maintenance and insurance, fuel, franchise/licence fees, accountancy fees, professional memberships, pension scheme, holiday and sick pay, and other expenses) would also have to be taken out of the income.

FRANCHISE FEES

Although the fee for trainers working through a franchise or business licence has fallen in recent years, you can still expect to pay in the region of £200 a week. In return, you will be provided with a new car, usually with only pre-delivery inspection mileage. You might, however, be supplied with a new car that has had some previous use. Contracts will stipulate that the trainer pays for all fuel used. Some franchise agreements will require a compulsory deposit or "car-bond", which may be part-refundable. Also, an extra charge can be made for each new customer provided. This can be in the region of £20 to £40. A new customer can be at any stage of training, from beginner to someone who is ready to take a driving test.

Some driving schools offer trainers what they call a "headboard franchise". This is where, for a weekly fee and minimum term contract, the school provides a headboard sporting their business details, business cards, posters, and promotional leaflets/flyers. The school will normally offer a limited flow of enquiries, leads, or actual new learners. The fee may be waived or reduced if less than the agreed minimum number of learners is supplied, though there can be penalties for late or missing franchise payments. Any new referrals from these learners will help you to build your business. When weighing up the risk, you will need to factor in the cost of your own training vehicle. Whatever business model or scheme you decide to follow, the potential earnings are ultimately dependent on your popularity with customers, along with your ability to understand the business and make it work for you.

WORK ON YOUR OWN OR WITH A DRIVING SCHOOL

Most driver trainers are self-employed, working freelance as sole traders. Many do work under what is called a "franchise", although it might be more accurate to describe it as a "business licence", where you are permitted to use a company name such as AA, BSM or RED Driving School. The British Franchise Association (BFA) does not recognise driving school "franchises", though the business model has some close similarities with those used in the "business to business" (B2B) and "business to consumer" (B2C) fields, within both blue and white-collar industries.

To take out a driving school franchise, you will have to agree to and sign a contract with the owner. Great caution needs to be exercised here, especially where the contract lasts over a year. In the event of any dispute, you will be held to this contract for the duration of its term. This will govern the use of any car supplied, along with the use of promotional materials and any intellectual property provided.

SMALL PRINT

Driving Schools will have a terms and conditions agreement for their customers. This will make the rules clear, ensuring lesson pre-payments and a lesson fee cancellation policy. If you work for yourself, you will need the same. You can get help and advice on this area by being a member of one of the industry's trade organisations.

CHAPTER 5

HOW LEARNERS LEARN TO DRIVE

Successful learning

When I hear, I forget.
When I see, I remember.
When I do, I understand.

This old Chinese proverb represents the senses, and their importance in our learning process. The five senses of seeing, hearing, touching, smelling, and tasting are the primary means we use to gain new knowledge. We rarely experience with one sense alone, so our senses work together to give us a total picture of our experiences, our surroundings, and our actions.

People of all ages learn best when involved in meaningful experiences. Learning takes place when the mind can focus information from all the senses and make connections with any previous learning. We remember 90% of all we do, 50% of all we see, but only 10% of all we hear. So, this suggests that best practice for driver trainers is to keep the lesson active and visual. In the context of learning to drive a car, the sense of touch (the feel for driving)—for example when moving off, changing speed by using the accelerator, gears, and brakes correctly—is particularly important for controlling the car safely and correctly.

THE LEARNING PROCESS: FROM INCOMPETENCE TO COMPETENCE

If the learning process is properly structured using regular lessons, then it is more likely to be successful. You choose when a subject needs explanation, demonstration, and the level of instruction for practice according to a student's level of ability at any given point. You also determine the type and number of questions to ask and when to ask them.

Learning is best achieved when topics are taught from what is known, to what is unknown. A popular way of looking at how a learner gains skill is the "Conscious Competence" learning model. In brief:

1. Unconscious incompetence: "I don't know what I don't know."
The learner does not understand or know how to drive. They are not aware of how much there is to learn to become a competent driver.

2. Conscious incompetence: "Ahh, there's something I don't know."
The learner recognises the skills needed in order to drive a car. The making of mistakes can be integral to the learning process. Plenty of encouragement needs to be given.

3. Conscious competence: "I can do this when I'm deliberate about it."
The learner understands or knows how to do something. Performing the skill requires concentration. There is significant conscious effort to execute the new skill.

4. Unconscious competence: "I can do this without even thinking."
The learner can drive competently. Sufficient practice means the skill has become second nature and can be performed easily.

One example to demonstrate this competence model, when learning to drive a manual car, is how to use the gearbox correctly. For example:

i.   At first you do not know what the gears are or how to use them (Unconscious incompetence).

ii.   You find out the benefits of the gearbox and how to use the lever in coordination with the clutch. You begin to practise, but make mistakes (Conscious incompetence).

iii.   With focus and concentration, you make no mistakes (Conscious competence).

iv.   With practice, you can change gears effortlessly as though on autopilot and, at the same time, perform other driving tasks successfully (Unconscious competence).

As the driver develops in the "unconscious competence" phase, there is the potential danger of familiarity breeding contempt and complacency. For instance, in forward planning, the new driver begins to take calculated risks such as crossing traffic signals as they turn red. Drivers can begin to drive "on memory" rather than "on sight". Also, as our perception of improved roads and better cars make us feel safer, we may be liable to take more risks.

These are issues to keep in mind when adapting the lesson plans to each learner's stage of ability, and there is plenty of work for the trainer to do to ensure that learners earn their Certificate of Competence to Drive at the first attempt. Learners who fail their test generally do so because they are insufficiently prepared.

On average, people who pass their driving test have had 47 hours of driving lessons with a professional trainer, along with 20 hours of private practise. The actual number of lessons needed to achieve competence will depend on the individual learner's ability, along with the frequency and length of lessons. Research indicates that where learners combine professional lessons with private practise, there is less risk of a serious collision happening after passing the test.

HOW TO ADAPT TEACHING TO A LEARNING STYLE

Teaching may come naturally to you. By recognising and understanding learning styles, we can adapt our teaching methods and techniques to suit everyone. This will improve the speed and quality of their learning. In short, we need to get the best balance of these:

1. **Eyes.** Keeping things visual, for instance by using diagrams or pictures.

2. **Ears.** Providing suitable explanations and using listening skills.

3. **Body.** Getting a feeling for the movement of the car.

4. **Hands and feet.** For instance, when using the car's controls.

One of the most popular ways of determining someone's learning style is to use a "Honey and Mumford" questionnaire. Briefly, the student is presented with a series of statements to which a response of 'agree' or 'disagree' is necessary. For instance:

• I have a reputation for having a no-nonsense, direct style.

• I am attracted more to new, unusual ideas, than to practical ones.

• Most times I believe the end justifies the means.

- I quickly get bored with methodical, detailed work.

- Flippant people who cannot take things seriously usually irritate me.

- I usually judge other people's ideas on their practical merits.

- I think that decisions based on the analysis of the information are sounder than those based on intuition.

- I prefer to respond to events spontaneously, rather than planning things out in advance.

- On balance, I tend to talk more than I should and need to develop my listening skills.

- I prefer to do the listening rather than the talking.

- I enjoy communicating my ideas and opinions to others.

- I enjoy the drama and excitement of a crisis.

There are no right or wrong responses. The answers will give some indication about which learning style(s) predominates:

1. **Activists** like to learn by being hands-on and doing something. They have a very practical approach to learning.

2. **Theorists** like to learn by understanding the theory. They like facts and to analyse them, drawing out new information using logic and reasoning.

3. **Pragmatists** like to put the learning into practice in the real world, by problem solving and discussing things.

4. **Reflectors** like to learn by observing and thinking about what happened. They prefer to stand back and view experiences from different perspectives, taking time to come to an appropriate conclusion.

There are several academic theories about how people learn. This model of learning styles is based on David Kolb's "Experiential Learning" cycle. The benefit of looking at this, is that it helps to improve the way that we deliver lesson content to each individual learner, matching them to their own appropriate style.

As an example, on a driving lesson where the learner is more of an "activist", the amount of briefing needed may be minimal. Most practical driving faults would be dealt with on the move. However, where the learner is more of a "theorist", then any briefing might need to be a little longer. With theorists, you should consider pulling up at the roadside more often in order to review the relevant learning points.

CHAPTER 6

HOW TO TEACH DRIVING

Successful teaching

Learning to drive is a serious business, but it should also be an enjoyable one that can have light-hearted moments. The correct balance needs to be found, and this will vary from learner to learner.

So, what are we teaching, and how?

Road safety is our business, and something is wrong. People in the 17–24 age group who have recently passed their driving tests are at much higher risk of having a collision than other groups of drivers. Traffic collision statistics show that one in five newly qualified drivers are at risk of serious crash within the first year of passing their driving test. The risk of young male drivers having collisions is greater than for females. Why? Well, as mentioned, if you ask a learner what they want to achieve, the vast majority will tell you they want to pass the test. The problem being that this alone is not enough to achieve safe driving for life.

Driving a car requires three areas of learning. These are:

1. **Physical skill**. How to control the car safely.

2. **Thinking skill**. Applying the "Highway Code" correctly to traffic situations.

3. **Attitude**. A permanent commitment to a defensive driving mind-set.

ADIs are good at delivering the first two areas of learning. However, something is missing. Researchers repeat the message that inexperienced drivers do not crash because of a lack of skill or knowledge, but because they make bad decisions. An obvious example is mobile phone use when driving: taking calls, texting, and using various apps causes a major distraction. Another is succumbing to peer pressure and driving too fast for the conditions, tailgating to push others in front to do the same, or continuing through red light signals, "because there's little risk of getting caught". The new young driver generally has a brain that is still developing (the frontal lobe "risk taking" matures at the age of 23 for females, 25 for males). Therefore, they struggle to realise the potential unseen danger. The perceived gain exceeds the risks, making this bad behaviour feel worthwhile or even fun. In addition, the potential "ripple effect" of responding to another driver's aggression or reckless behaviour can cause a terrible chain of events, which heighten the risk of an injury or fatal collision.

Behaviour is not the same as skill. Behaviour is influenced by motives, attitudes, and emotional responses to traffic and other road users. Driving is a way to express our personality, and sometimes this can happen in an amplified way. People who enjoy taking risks in life may well take greater risks when driving. Anti-social risk taking when driving results in poor style, minimal attention to the road, and reduced vehicle stability. The outcome is a high risk of collision involvement.

The challenge for the ADI is to teach in a way that has a permanent influence on the new driver's behaviour after passing the driving test. Changing a person's mindset may be difficult, but it is not impossible. Lodging in them an awareness of the bigger picture and the potential consequences provides them with the internal opportunity to balance risk and common sense, with the practical realities in the short-term. An example of this in the wider social field is how attitudes towards smoking have changed dramatically in recent decades. Smoking at work or on public transport is unthinkable today, but it was once the norm in everyday life for many of us.

Can driver trainers realistically meet this challenge? If so, how are they going to adapt their teaching? How do we point the way forward? The "Goals for Driver Education" (GDE Matrix) combined with the DVSA's "Car and Light Van Driving Syllabus" are the industry's answer, formed over many years through academic and scientific research and practical professional evidence.

GOALS FOR DRIVER EDUCATION

GDE provides a summary for trainers of what needs to be addressed during the teaching process, to produce safe and responsible drivers. Correct use will enhance and improve the quality of our teaching and the learner's learning and understanding. These goals are set out as a matrix of four levels and three competencies:

Goals for Driver Education (GDE Matrix)			
The 4 Levels	Knowledge and skill to master	Risk-increasing factors	Self-evaluation
1. Mastery of vehicle control and manoeuvring	The physics of driving, handling when braking, accelerating, and steering.	Risks connected with advanced vehicle technology. Distraction through smart phone use.	Strengths and weaknesses with basic driving skills when manoeuvring through hazards.
2. Mastery of traffic situations	General driving knowledge and skills. Applying "Highway Code". Observation and anticipation.	Disobeying rules. Awareness of vulnerable road user. Adverse driving or traffic conditions.	Level of hazard perception, from a viewpoint of strengths and weaknesses.
3. Goals and context of driving	Purpose and need for the journey. Route planning. Amount of driving time.	Driver's physiological condition. Peer pressures. Traffic—rural/urban, day/night.	How well has the trip been planned? What are the goals, motives, feelings, and expectations?
4. Goals for life and skills for living	Behavioural style and how this affects your driving.	Risks connected with social/peer pressure to perform a particular way. Lifestyle habits that create driving risk.	Attitude. Risk tendencies: Impulse control, motives, fatigue, stress, lifestyle and values, coping strategy.
This matrix can help trainers teach learners to think more about others on the road, and how to avoid a high-risk driving style.			

To measure learning outcomes, any agreed goal needs to be "SMART" (Specific, Measurable, Achievable in a Realistic Timeframe).

The framework is NOT a stepped approach to driver training, where the learner begins at Level 1 and then graduates sequentially through Levels 2 and 3 up to 4. Rather, it is a way of using the higher levels to influence the lower levels. How we control the car (Level 1) and drive in traffic (Level 2) is a direct result of the motive for the journey (Level 3) and our personality (Level 4). Also, the degree to which we can self-evaluate (Column 3) will directly affect the control we have over the vehicle (Level 1), how we interact with other road users (Level 2), the choices we make about the journey (Level 3), the degree of responsibility and control we have over our own lives, and therefore the driving task (Level 4).

Where the driver trainer concentrates solely on the first two levels, this will continue to produce the conditioned behaviour expected to pass the driving test. To help introduce the other two critical levels, an exercise would be to map the GDE Matrix with the DVSA's national driving syllabus and standards.

DRIVER AND VEHICLE STANDARDS AGENCY (DVSA) CAR AND LIGHT VAN DRIVING SYLLABUS (LICENCE CATEGORY B)

The DVSA syllabus sits alongside the "National Standard for Driving Cars and Light Vans". It outlines, in an NVQ (National Vocational Qualification) format, the competencies needed for safe and responsible driving. In other words, it identifies the skills, knowledge, and understanding required to be a safe and responsible driver of a Licence Category B vehicle (a car).

For the driver trainer, the "National Standard" provides reference material that details good practice for driver training. It is up to each individual trainer to decide how to deliver the learning outcomes. The full document can easily be found with an internet search. There will be different, valid ways to deliver the learning outcomes, but ultimately the trainer decides.

It would be wrong to expect all driver trainers to know every minute detail in the "National Standard". Similarly, it is not necessary to know the GDE Matrix inside and out to do a brilliant job. What does matter, is that driver trainers self-evaluate the importance of both, understand the central tenets, and incorporate this understanding into their teaching methods.

CLIENT CENTRED LEARNING (CCL)

We need to think about the type of lesson delivery that will suit each individual learner driver. Our teaching style needs to match individual learning styles such as "activist" or "theorist". If the road safety issue highlighted at the beginning of this chapter is to be addressed, the learning process needs to be interactive. This contrasts with traditional driving instruction, where the learner is simply told what to do. With this passive, "expert knows best approach", learning, understanding, and retention is much more likely to be short-term and limited. A lesson that focuses on driving faults, associated with the pass/fail driving test criteria, is inevitably a negative learning experience. Also, relying too much on route learning techniques, where the trainer uses repetitive practise, is also fairly ineffective for the longer-term "safe driving for life".

Client Centred Learning (CCL) assumes that the professional trainer-learner relationship is based on equality, believing that more learning is achieved by the learner forming their own understanding, rather than relying solely on a transfer of information and knowledge from the trainer. The trainer-learner relationship is non-judgemental, allowing the learner to feel comfortable expressing opinion. From the earliest opportunity, learners should take active responsibility and ownership for their learning process.

During modern driving lessons, learners are encouraged to engage in an active role. While driving, suitable opportunities will arise where the trainer can use one or more scenarios as a learning point. When reviewing these, a reflective approach will help gain an insight into the learner's views, values, beliefs, and understanding.

Whatever the learner's personality; judgment and decisions made when driving are shaped by a variety of influences. These include skill and knowledge, personal confidence to act, the opinions and attitudes of our friends, colleagues, peers, other learners, and the values and norms which operate in wider society. Any of these factors can have a direct impact on the decisions that learners make when learning to drive, and when they become qualified/drive unaccompanied.

All that being said, it would be a misconception to think that CCL is about letting the learner make all the decisions. The trainer retains full control of the lesson, bringing essential experience and expertise to the learning process. It is not client-led learning, more "client-focused" learning.

COACHING SKILLS

Put simply, telling isn't learning.

Former racing driver, Sir John Whitmore, author of "Coaching for Performance" described coaching as a way of managing, a way of treating people, a way of thinking, and a way of being. Developing coaching skills is believed to produce a far deeper level of learning and understanding than if the new driver was purely instructed. In recent years, the term "coaching" has gradually moved from sport into all types of training and development. We should consider the difference between coaching and instruction, and how we can effectively use both when teaching learners:

- **Instruction**. This is split into full or guided instruction. When we are dealing with a complete novice or partly-trained learner, we need to instruct them until they, firstly gain confidence and, secondly remember what to do and when to do it. We are teaching them to learn a new skill. As training continues, instruction is still important for safety critical situations.

  Instruction, albeit subconsciously, can be test-focused and fault orientated. It is unlikely to deal with post-test scenarios and is not so effective in engaging learners into understanding high-risk, anti-social behaviours.

- **Coaching**. Learning more by suggestion. When matched to the learner's level of ability, it can prove to be part of an effective fault correction technique. Coaching uses self-evaluation to encourage more ownership and responsibility for better driving as a life skill.

Coaching uses the "Question-and-Answer" technique; asking questions to produce answers that develop and show what the learner thinks and feels, active listening, feedback techniques, rapport building, and the use of the coach's intuition to help learners raise awareness through their own guided thought development. By discovering the answers themselves, learners retain that information more effectively over the long-term.

Sir John Whitmore, in his book, *Coaching for Performance* takes the coaching framework a step further with the "GROW Model". "GROW" is an acronym for the four key steps in coaching:

Goals. Goals and aspirations (What do you want?). Setting a goal is an important part of coaching. Goals provide us with something against which we can measure progress and aim to achieve. Getting the goal right can be a challenge, because if the goal is too difficult then it can be counterproductive. However, if the goal is not sufficiently challenging, the learner may not progress.

Reality. Current situation, internal and external obstacles (Where are you now?). In this element of the GROW model, the aim is to encourage the learner to identify the reality of where they are in relation to achieving their goals. This stage of the model can provide a useful recap of the main learning points from the previous training, and any accompanied driver training.

Options. Possibilities, strengths, and resources (What could you do?). This stage of the model is, in many ways, the key to the coaching model. The aim for the driving coach here is to encourage the learner to consider a number of options that could further develop their performance. The driving coach should ask the student to think about several possible options, and then explore the benefits and disadvantages of each.

Will. Actions and accountability (What will you do?). In this stage of the model, the learner is asked to select an option that they feel would work for them. Once the learner has selected the option, the driving coach would enquire as to why they felt that the selected option would work, and how they would know if it was successful. This is an important part of the process, particularly when the situation being discussed cannot easily be duplicated in a lesson.

The idea behind "GROW" is to encourage problem solving, goal setting, and performance improvement, not from above by the expert, but from "within" the learner's own mind. However, you should remember that learners may want to be told what to do! If a learner wishes to be only told what to do, we must respect this, whilst also recognising that it can present a disadvantage on a driving test, because they are less able to make good judgements in challenging situations. Because coaching encourages the taking of responsibility for learning and their actions, this approach has a better chance of helping the driver to pass, and conducting themselves safely on the road after passing. As driver trainers, we want our learners to stay safe when driving unaccompanied post-test. The client-centred approach really helps with this, as our coaching skills are blended with the higher levels of the GDE Matrix.

Many ADIs continue what they have always done previously. That is, to adopt a driving test fault-focused approach to the training they deliver. The previous DVSA ADI training standards were probably a culprit for this. Likewise, customer pressure to be trained by what the "examiner expects on a driving test" was not helpful. Today's thinking is that such an approach is outdated, and does little for long-term road safety. When the Driver Trainer realises the true difference between training people to drive and summative assessment, then the teaching of learners improves and road safety benefits.

Easy? Maybe not! To develop the ideas contained in this chapter on a practical level, it is worth joining and participating in professional association workshops, webinars, conferences, and other training and CPD events. Information on these is readily available online.

CHAPTER 7

HOW TO QUALIFY AS A DVSA APPROVED DRIVING INSTRUCTOR (ADI)

Can I pass these exams?

You cannot teach a person to drive for payment or reward unless you have been officially registered to do so. For anyone wishing to qualify as a driving trainer, the Driving and Vehicle Standards Agency (DVSA) is the awarding body. To become an ADI, you must pass a three-part entry examination with the DVSA to become registered.

Around 70% of people that begin the registration process, will drop out or fail to qualify. Undoubtedly, much of the high failure rate is down to entrants into the process having failed to research what is involved, especially the time and cost. As with anything in life, research and preparation is the key to securing success. With a good view of the training road ahead, along with the employment of a good driving instructor trainer or enrolment onto a reputable training course, most candidates will be perfectly capable of achieving professional success.

The Register of Approved Driving Instructors (ADI) was introduced in October 1964 on a voluntary basis. Newly qualified instructors could claim the title of "Ministry of Transport Approved Driving Instructor". From October 1970, this registration became compulsory. Today's qualification is known as "Driver Vehicle Standards Agency Approved Driving Instructor". Choice of training provider should be made very carefully. There is a voluntary scheme administered by the DVSA that lists approximately 300 inspected businesses on the "Official Register of Driving Trainer Training (ORDIT) Establishments", using some 600 instructor trainers. The DVSA estimates that 75% of potential driving instructors use trainers who are ORDIT registered. Contact details for these ORDIT registered establishments can be found at: www.gov.uk.

Any training you undertake should build on your driving and communication skills experience. This is likely to focus mainly on the technical skills you need to demonstrate to pass the DVSA's three-part qualifying examination. The DVSA not only conduct the qualifying examination, but they also supervise driver trainers once they have qualified. Regular "Standards Checks" are undertaken every few years, to ensure a driver trainer is achieving professional standards. A performance grade is given at the end of each check, and this determines the period before the next assessment check.

It may be some time since you took any form of public examination. You need to find someone who knows the format well and who has the experience and understanding to adapt to your own learning style, ultimately building your confidence and skillset. If you know someone who can recommend an ADI Trainer, then this is a good next step. As with all training, finding the trainer or training provider that suits you is key to making the learning process as enjoyable, efficient, and successful as possible.

The three-part ADI qualifying examination:

1. **Part One: Your knowledge.** This is a computer-based theory test that includes multiple-choice questions along with a hazard perception test using video media.

2. **Part Two: A driving test.** This is an enhanced practical test of your own driving ability using a manual car.

3. **Part Three: An instructional ability test.** This is a practical test of your instructional ability, where the examiner observes you giving a driving lesson.

You must pass each part before taking the next. You can sit the theory test as many times as you need to, but you are limited to three attempts at the practical test within two years of passing part one. You will need to show your UK photocard driving licence for each test.

Consider how you will study and best prepare for each part. Think about how you relate the multiple-choice questions, including hazard perception video clips, to the two practical parts that will follow.

HOW TO PASS PART ONE

The pass rate for this part, is around 50%. Part one begins with a knowledge test lasting a maximum of 90 minutes. Using a computer, you will be asked 100 questions and will have a choice of four possible answers for each question. This will be followed by a hazard perception test using a total of 14 video clips. You will need to click the mouse or tap a key on the keyboard each time you see a "developing hazard".

On the multiple-choice questions, you must score at least 85% overall and a minimum of 20 out of 25 in each of four question bands. These are:

1. Road Procedure

2. Car Control and Vehicle Mechanics

3. Motoring Law, Disabilities, and the Driving Test

4. Publications and Instructional Techniques

Practice questions that cover the learning points are commercially available from the DVSA and other publishers.

Potential trainers need up-to-date foundation knowledge, combined with an understanding of driving. The most important publications to study are:

- *The Highway Code* (available online as a free download)

- *Driving: The Essential Skills* (available online as a purchase)

It is also important to be totally familiar with:

- *Know Your Traffic Signs* (available online as a free download)

The hazard perception test consists of 14 video clips. Each clip features everyday road scenes and contains at least one "developing hazard". One of the clips features two developing hazards. The skill is to spot developing hazards immediately. For reference, a developing hazard is an event that would cause you, as a driver, to respond with a reactive change of speed or direction. For example, a car is parked on the left-hand side of the road. This vehicle becomes a developing hazard as soon as the right-turn indicator starts to flash and it begins to move off. You can score up to five points for each developing hazard.

To get a maximum score, click the mouse as soon as you see the hazard starting to develop. You do not lose points if you click and get it wrong. However, you will not score anything if you click continuously or in a pattern. The maximum score that can be achieved is 75 points. To achieve this, you need to anticipate every developing hazard as early as possible. The minimum pass score is 57.

For preparation, the DVSA recommend the *Driving Instructor's Handbook* by John Miller. This is a comprehensive reference book. If you plan to buy this, make sure that you purchase the latest edition. It can be bought online through Amazon or through any good high street bookshops.

Distance learning packages are available from training organisations, though most potential driver trainers purchase their study materials online and manage their own studies at a pace and time convenient to themselves.

HOW TO PASS PART TWO

This part of the testing process is an assessment of your driving ability, and the pass rate is around 60%. You will need to provide your own vehicle, but the DVSA have some rules governing what types of car you can or cannot use on driving tests. For instance, you cannot use a convertible, and your vehicle cannot be fitted with a "space saver" tyre. It will need to be fitted with an adjustable rear-view mirror for the examiner's use, and have an easily adjustable seat with a head restraint for a forward-facing front passenger. Broadly speaking, the car must be legal, roadworthy, and capable of normal performance for vehicles of its type. Your test will be cancelled and you will have to pay again if your car does not meet the rules. Please check for further details and updates at www.gov.uk.

Manual and automatic cars

If you have a manual licence, you can take the test in either a manual or automatic car. You will be able to train people in both types of car when you have qualified. If you have an automatic licence, you must take the test in an automatic car. You will only be able to train people in an automatic car when you have qualified.

What happens during the test?

Part two lasts around an hour, and is in five parts:

1. An eyesight check.

2. "Show me, tell me" vehicle safety questions.

3. General driving ability.

4. Manoeuvres.

5. Independent driving.

The eyesight test. You must be able to read a new-style vehicle number plate from a distance of at least 26.5 metres. New-style number plates start with two letters followed by two numbers, such as AB51 ABC. Where the vehicle is fitted with an old-style plate, the minimum distance is 27.5 metres.

You will fail the test if you do not pass the eyesight test. This would count as one of the three attempts you are allowed at the ADI Part Two test.

Vehicle safety questions. The examiner will ask a total of five questions relating to basic vehicle maintenance and knowledge; three "tell me" questions at the start of your test/ before you start driving, and two "show me" questions while you are driving—for example, showing how to wash the windscreen by operating the wiper control.

- A driving fault is recorded for each incorrect answer and a serious fault is marked if you answer all five questions incorrectly.

Your general driving ability. This will last approximately one hour, and forms the majority of part two. You are expected to drive as an experienced motorist, demonstrating the best practices of road safety, and not like a good learner. While the standard for a "pass" is referred to as "advanced", the thinking behind the assessment criteria is more in keeping with the DVSA's publication *Driving: The Essential Skills*, rather than the police driver's handbook, *Roadcraft*. You will have to show the examiner all of the following:

- Expert handling of the controls.
- Use of correct road procedure.

- Anticipation of the actions of other road users and then taking appropriate action.

- Sound judgement of distance, speed, and timing.

- Consideration for the convenience and safety of other road users.

- Driving in an environmentally friendly manner.

You will drive in varying road and traffic conditions, including motorways or dual carriageways where possible. There will be a 20-minute period of independent driving, where the examiner will choose either of the following:

- **Directions from a sat nav.** When following directions from a sat nav, the examiner will provide the sat nav and set it up for you. You cannot follow directions from your own sat nav during the test.

- **Traffic signs.** If you cannot see a traffic sign, for instance, because it is covered by trees, the examiner will give you directions until you can see the next one.

The examiner will tell you which you have to do. You might also be asked to carry out an emergency stop.

The examiner will ask you to demonstrate two of the following reversing exercises:

- Parallel park at the side of the road.

- Reverse into a parking bay and drive out.

- Drive into a parking bay and reverse out.

- Pull up on the right-hand side of the road, reverse for around two car lengths, and re-join the traffic.

Your test result will not be affected if you take a wrong turning, unless you make a fault while doing it. The examiner will help you get back on route if you do.

If you make mistakes during your test, it might not affect your test result, providing said errors are not serious. Your driving examiner will direct you back to the driving test centre if the mistake you made means you have failed, and the test will end early.

During the examiner's assessment, there are three types of faults that can be marked:

1. **A dangerous fault** involves actual danger to you, the examiner, the public, or property.

2. **A serious fault** could potentially be dangerous

3. **A driving fault** might not be potentially dangerous, but if you make the same fault throughout your test it could become a serious fault.

You will pass the test if you make:

- No more than six driving faults.

- No serious or dangerous faults.

TRAINEE LICENCE

Having passed the first parts of the ADI exams, you can opt to join the trainee licensing scheme. This is an optional licence valid for six months, known in the industry as the "Pink Badge". This must be displayed along the nearside edge of the windscreen, low in the bottom corner, when giving paid driving lessons.

Although this licence is not compulsory, the teaching practice and experience should help you achieve success with part three. You will need to be sponsored by a driving school that will oversee the compulsory training you will need to take. This amounts to a minimum of 40 hours pre-licence training, along with a further 20 hours before your first attempt at part three. Further elements of five hours will be necessary, before you re-attempt the test. The examiner will ask for written proof of the training at the beginning of the next part of the test.

HOW TO PASS PART THREE

The pass rate here is around 35%. This is a test of your instructional technique, and will again last about an hour. The same rules for the car used apply here, and if your car does not meet the rules, your test will be cancelled and you will have to pay again.

If you have a manual licence, you can take the test in either a manual or automatic car. You will be able to train people in both types of car when you have qualified. If you have an automatic licence, you must take the test in an automatic car. You will only be able to train people in an automatic car when you have qualified.

Here, the examiner will observe you giving a real, live driving lesson with one of your learners. This should be time managed so that it lasts no longer than an hour. Your learner can be either:

- Partly trained.
- Fully trained.
- A full licence holder.

Your learner should **not** be an absolute beginner who has just started learning to drive.

At the beginning of the lesson, briefly discuss and agree the goals for the lesson and risk management with your learner. During the lesson, your performance will be assessed on your ability to:

1. Lesson plan.
2. Manage risk.
3. Show teaching and learning strategies.

Your teaching should show association with the national standard for driver training.

At the end of the lesson, you will need time to reflect and recap the lesson with the learner, and/or discuss their performance. When assessing performance, trainers are awarded a score from 0 to 3 for each of 17 competencies associated with the categories above. You will automatically fail if you get a score of 7 or less in the "risk management" category, or where the examiner stops the lesson because you have put the vehicle or someone else in danger.

After you have given the lesson, the examiner will discuss your performance and give you your result. You will receive your grade, along with your completed ADI Part Three test report form.

Total Score	Grade	Description
0-30	Fail	Your performance is unsatisfactory. Your name will not be entered onto the ADI Register.
31-42	Grade B	You can apply to join the ADI Register.
43-51	Grade A	You have shown a high standard of instruction and you will be allowed to apply to join the ADI Register.

Once you have passed all three parts of the exam process, you will be fully qualified and will need to apply for your registration certificate, known as the "Green Badge". When giving lessons, this must be displayed along the nearside edge of your windscreen, low in the bottom corner.

You must apply to join the register within one year of passing. To retain your registration, you must be available to have one lesson supervised periodically, at the registrar's request. This is known as the "Standards Check" and, again, you will be assessed giving a real lesson.

HOW LONG WILL IT TAKE TO QUALIFY?

This depends on both your own learning ability and the availability of tests from the DVSA.

You must pass the three tests separately within a two-year time limit. If you do not pass within this time frame, you will need to start again from the beginning. Do not take any test until you know what is involved, have had sufficient preparation and training, and genuinely believe you have reached test standard.

The waiting period for all tests depends on the demand in your area. From first applying to register, you can expect the process of qualifying to take a minimum of a year.

HOW HARD ARE THE ADI TESTS?

After reading the information and detail in this guide, you will have a good idea of how difficult or easy each test might prove to be for you. You should ensure that you take at least one mock or simulated test when you have completed each stage of your training. Act on any feedback or other advice before you take the real thing. If necessary, you should postpone your test; do not take a test purely for the experience of doing so.

Taking a mock test for part one is easy using software and apps that are readily available. In terms of practising for part two, an experienced ORDIT trainer will be able to simulate this test for you. There is some merit in taking one of the many advanced driving tests available as a precursor to part two, but do be mindful that the assessment criteria is slightly different, and based on *Roadcraft* rather than *Driving: The Essential Skills*.

There is probably much more to becoming a qualified driving trainer than you expected, but no test is difficult if you are properly prepared! Some candidates will need more time to get ready, especially for part three. However, if you have teaching experience already, this will undoubtedly help you. If not, then getting some teaching practice on a trainee licence will probably be of benefit for you. The best preparation will be for your ORDIT trainer to supervise the driving lessons you give, where you have an agreement with your learners.

WHAT ARE THE COSTS INVOLVED?

You will need to pay fees to the DVSA for each of the three tests, and for your licences. The DVSA fees are subject to change. Currently, they are as follows:

Exam Part / Licence	What is it?	Cost
Disclosure and Barring Service (DBS)	This is a check whether you have any criminal convictions, spent or unspent.	£6
Identity Check	This check is made at a crown post office.	£6
ADI Part One	ADI Part One ADI Registration. Includes CRB check and one attempt at the combined theory and hazard perception test.	£81
ADI Part Two	A one-hour "advanced" driving test.	£111
Trainee Licence	Optional six-month licence for teaching practice, "Pink Badge".	£140
ADI Part Three	A one-hour instructional ability test,	£111
ADI Licence	ADI Licence Full licence, renewable every four years. "Green Badge".	£300
Total DVSA Fees	**With** Trainee Licence	**£755**
	Without Trainee Licence	**£615**

ADI TRAINING FEES

These will depend on your choice of training provider and will vary considerably. You need to ensure that you choose a trainer who is on the Official Register of Driving Trainer Training (ORDIT) list. My advice is that conducting your own research before committing yourself to any agreement, will be time well-spent. Make full and frank enquiries as to the cost, what is provided, and what happens if you are not successful. Some providers will charge by the lesson, which is often an hour in duration. Others may charge a block fee for the entire course, or part thereof. You need to find out who is the best within your own locality and, again, research cannot be overemphasised. Perhaps contact local ADIs or the local ADI Association, or speak to someone at one of the national ADI associations for advice.

APPLYING TO BECOME A DRIVER TRAINER

You have to be at least 21 years old. You must also have held a full car licence for at least three years before you can apply to the Driver and Vehicle Standards Agency (DVSA) to become an Approved Driver Instructor (ADI).

It is easy to apply online at www.gov.uk, as the website will walk you through the application process. This begins with a Disclosure and Barring Service (DBS) Standard and Enhanced Check. You will need your driving licence and national insurance number for this. Later on, you will need to provide proof of your identity to a crown post office who will, for a counter fee, check your ID and inform the DVSA's contractor.

Driver Trainers are in a position of considerable trust. To become an ADI, the law says that you must be a "fit and proper" person. Because it does not define what this means, the ADI Registrar interprets failure to achieve this set standard as "the personal and professional standards, conduct or behaviour that could be unacceptable in the eyes of the public and other ADIs". The ADI Registrar assesses the risk you are likely to pose to the public. For instance, if you have been convicted of a sexual, violent, financial, or drug-related crime, or banned from working with children, then you are likely to be refused.

The DVSA are also likely to refuse ADI applications where someone has:

- Five or more penalty points on their driving licence.

- Been banned from driving in the last four years.

- Been convicted of any non-motoring offences.

This chapter is intended for those who are looking to become driving trainers in the UK. If you are taking your test in Northern Ireland, the setup is similar, but you will need to check the website www.nidirect.gov.uk for details of any variations.

CHAPTER 8

HOW TO BECOME A 'GRADE A' DRIVER TRAINER

Aim High

Setting and Maintaining your Standards

We all want to be the best, even if we don't necessarily admit it. But, this is a good thing! Whether you're working in the driving industry, or somewhere else entirely, you should always strive to perform to the highest possible standard. When it comes to ADIs, achieving "Grade A" is an official recognition that you are performing to the best level.

Having said this, how much meaning does the grade have outside the industry? Arguably, when selling to the public, a friendly demeanour and a reputation for punctuality and reliability will do more to create new business than touting the top grade on the Standards Check.

The DVSA "Standards Check", introduced in April 2014 (like its predecessor the "Check Test") presents a snapshot assessment of our ability to teach. The same can be said for the driving test, where the candidate aims to give their best performance, with the objective of gaining their full driving licence and the freedom and independence that this allows. Therefore, to be sure of achieving Grade A in the DVSA Standards Check, we must ensure the training we provide is always to the highest possible standard.

This chapter is designed to help clarify what the official expectations are and what DVSA examiners have been trained to look for. The DVSA's "National Standards" set out the skills, knowledge, and understanding considered necessary for teaching learners. They use the "competencies" format that dominates vocational qualifications such as NVQ and BTEC awards. This expresses itself with outcomes, identified in terms of knowledge, understanding, and performance that an ADI needs to demonstrate. Remember that there may well be more than one way to achieve each of the stated outcomes.

The three main competencies against which the ADI is assessed are:

1. Lesson Planning
2. Risk Management
3. Teaching and Learning Strategies

These are broken down into 17 further competencies. When looking at the details, we will find some inevitable overlaps of the information provided.

LESSON PLANNING

Benjamin Franklin, one of the founding fathers of the United States of America, is credited to have said: 'By failing to prepare, you are preparing to fail.' In our context, we can express this as 'failing to plan, is planning to fail'. This is fundamental to the Standards Check.

To demonstrate the four listed competencies for lesson planning, trainers need to consider:

- How many hours or periods of training the learner has already had.

- Whether the learner is receiving any other practice, such as from parents or friends.

- The learner's strengths and weakness, forming "action points" for areas of further development.

- How the training route should be designed to help achieve agreed goals in the lesson.

If you have documentation for the learner's record of progress, including "reflective logs", show this to the Standards Check examiner before the start of the lesson. This can help clarify the goals to be achieved, plus your attention to and understanding of each individual learner.

It is also a good idea to ask each learner to scale their driving competencies from 1 to 10. Follow this by asking what they think they are best at, and what they have difficulties with. Listen to what they say and agree the learning goals, planning the training needs going forward and fitting these, as appropriate, into the lesson ahead. This should usually be a simple exercise that need not take too long.

If you have little or no experience of working with the learner, a short assessment to identify training needs will be necessary before finalising the lesson plan. It is impossible to structure the lesson correctly without agreeing the goals and needs of that particular lesson.

When it comes to practical training, an effective learning experience is judged to be one where the learner takes on as much responsibility as possible for their own learning. One example of this is to encourage learners to find the answer for themselves, rather than depending on being given the answer by you. Another example is to ask the learner to think through what might happen in certain situations, such as if the road and traffic conditions were different. For example, after negotiating a certain road or traffic hazard, it might be helpful to discuss the same event and how it may vary in difficulty and approach at peak times or in poor weather.

Should suitable opportunities arise for discussion between the trainer and the learner, questions can be used whilst on the move. These must be tailored to the learner's ability and should not create distraction from their driving task. Questions may be open or closed, goal or task specific, or safety critical. However, too many or any unnecessary questions can be de-motivating for the learner and possibly create a hazard or impede their driving ability.

Where a learner offers an inappropriate comment, for instance, about the behaviour of another road user, it would be correct for the ADI to challenge this.

RISK MANAGEMENT

These five competencies are concerned with the on-road management of any uncertainties, threats, or possible consequences of driving errors made by the learner or any other road user. Trainers are responsible for developing the learner's awareness and ability to manage road risk (as a key driver responsibility). At the same time, trainers must:

- Protect the learner and third parties from danger. It may be necessary to make a physical as well as verbal intervention to manage a safety critical incident. Not doing this will result in a failure of the Standards Check. You are supervising your student and therefore have overall responsibility for their safety, and the safety of other road users and pedestrians during a lesson.

Nevertheless, sharing basic responsibilities starts from the first lesson with a new untrained provisional licence holder.

Beginning with the "Controls Lesson", the trainer must explain the protocol for using the dual controls. As the lessons progress, any physical intervention will require a suitable review of the circumstances, including why it was necessary. Having achieved an understanding of what went wrong, the learner may be asked to repeat the exercise or manoeuvre again, with or without instruction or coaching. At this point, the ADI must ensure that the learner knows exactly what is expected of them.

- The "balance of responsibility", between the trainer and the learner varies according to their level of ability and individual circumstances. On a Standards Check, trainers should not assume that because the issue of risk management has been dealt with before the observed lesson, it is not necessary for the observed lesson and not subject to assessment. Risk management needs to be actively addressed during the check, for the benefit of the examiner.

All directions and instructions given by the ADI must be sufficient, timely and appropriate, taking the learner's level of ability into account. Directions given late, or in a confusing or misleading way, do not allow the learner to respond appropriately and can make weaknesses worse. Giving too many instructions at once may cause overload or confusion.

It should be obvious that a trainer must be in control of each driving lesson, though too much overt control can be viewed as a weakness. Lesson control includes the trainer having the skill to:

- Take in what is going on in the road ahead, to the sides, and behind the training vehicle.

- Observe the actions of the learner, including any remarks, as well as non-verbal communications.

- Judge whether those actions are suitable in any given circumstances.

Any necessary verbal or physical interventions must be timely and appropriate. In the moving-car environment, where a trainer remains silent, demonstrating positive body language suggests confidence in the learner; this is just as much a coaching input as asking questions.

The most important "interventions" are those that positively manage risk in a moving car. ADIs are expected to identify situations in which a risk or hazard might arise to their learner. On some occasions this will involve physical intervention by the ADI in order to prevent a situation escalating. To succeed on a Standards Check, trainers need to demonstrate an ability to:

- Intervene in a way that actively supports the learning process and safety during the session.

- Allow the learner to deal with situations within their ability.

- Take control of any situation where the learner is clearly out of their depth.

Where a safety critical or potentially critical incident occurs, the learner must fully understand what happened and how the circumstances could have been dealt with better at the time, or completely avoided. Ideally, the learner will be able to analyse the situation that occurred for themselves.

On a Standards Check, trainers need to demonstrate the ability to:

- Find a safe place to pull up, to review the critical incident.

- Allow the learner enough time to express any fears or concerns the incident may have caused.

- Support the learner to reflect clearly about what happened.

- Provide input to clarify aspects of the incident that the learner does not understand.

- Support the learner to identify strategies for future situations.

- Provide input where the learner does not understand what they should do differently.

- Check that the learner feels able to put the agreed strategy in place going forward.

- Agree ways of developing that competence, where the learner feels this need.

TEACHING AND LEARNING STRATEGIES

In our chapter "How to Teach Driving" we said that "learning to drive is a serious business, but it should also be an enjoyable one that can have its light-hearted moments". Remember, the correct balance needs to be found, and this will vary from learner to learner.

By reflecting on our teaching practice, we can determine what is working best, and with which learners in what circumstances. There's a lot of talk about "

Client-Centred Learning (CCL)", but what does this phrase mean to you? CCL is not a new strategy within this industry, but should be considered as a progressive option that helps ensure that new learning is more effective. The intention of CCL is to help achieve a higher level of understanding through self-directed solutions, for example, problem solving.

Teaching style

One size does not fit all. The trainer's teaching style needs to adapt to suit the learner and their level of ability.

Re-visit Chapter 6 in this book. How do you adapt your teaching style to each learner's own way of learning? For example, some learners will be very willing to learn actively as they go, while others may benefit from opportunities to reflect before making the next step in their learning.

Competence is demonstrated where a trainer:

- Actively works to understand how to best support the learner's way of learning.

- Modifies their teaching style when, or if, they realise there is a need to do so.

- Provides an accurate and technically correct demonstration, instruction, or information.

- Uses practical examples to provide a different way of looking at a particular subject.

- Links learning in theory to learning in practice.

- Encourages and helps the learner to take ownership of the learning process.

- Responds to driving faults in a timely manner.

- Provides enough uninterrupted time to practice new skills.

- Provides the learner with clear guidance about how they might practise outside the session.

Encouraging learners to "problem solve"

Where a trainer decides to give the learner a task to do, or an answer to come up with, then it's important that the learner is given enough time to do this. Different pupils will respond to such an invitation in various ways. Insisting that a learner should come up with an answer on the spot may well be unproductive for some.

Competence is demonstrated where a trainer:

- Provides time, in a suitable location, to explore any problems or issues that arose during the lesson or that were raised by the learner.

- Providing timely opportunities for analysis; promptly in the case of risk critical incidents.

- Taking time and using suitable techniques to understand any problems the learner had with understanding an issue.

- Suggesting suitable strategies to help the learner develop their understanding, such as using practical examples or pointing them at further reading.

- Giving clear and accurate information to fill gaps in the learner's knowledge or understanding.

- Leaving the learner feeling that they had responsibility for their learning in the situation.

Learning outcomes

These are what the learner will "know" or "be able to do" within a defined period. The DVSA's national standard for "Safe and Responsible Driving (Category B)" provides all the required "learning outcomes". In this standard, the requirements are expressed as statements. If you search the internet and download the document, you will see that each element is divided into "Performance Standards" (Practical) and "Knowledge and Understanding" (Theory). One example from the standard is:

Unit 2.2 Drive the vehicle safely and responsibly	
Element 2.2.1 Monitor and respond to information from instrumentation, driving aids and the environment.	
Performance Standards	Knowledge & Understanding requirements
You must be able to:	You must know and understand:
• Make effective use of mirrors and other aids to vision to identify and monitor other road users and hazards.	• How different types of mirror can make other road users appear to be nearer or further away than they actually are.

Competence is demonstrated where a trainer:

- Uses practical examples identified on a lesson in a suitable way and at a suitable time, to confirm or reinforce understanding.

- Explores different ways to use practical examples to respond to differences in the preferred learning style.

- Uses practical examples that are within the learner's range of experience and ability to understand.

- Recognises that some learners will be able to respond instantly, while others will want to think about the issue before responding.

Technical information

This needs to be accurate, relevant, and given in a timely manner. A failure to meet any one of these criteria on a Standards Check will cause the other competencies in this group to become redundant. Most sessions will require some technical input from the ADI to help the learner solve problems or to fill a gap in their knowledge.

Where a recurring weakness is identified in the learner's driving, it is not enough to simply tell the learner that they have done something wrong. Nothing has been taught until it has been learnt, so the ADI must ensure learner understanding. For example, informing the learner that 'you're too close to these parked cars' could be used to introduce further coaching on a weakness. How close is "too close"? Why is the learner too close? Where is the learner looking, and where should they be looking? Should the car be moving at a slower speed? Questioning the learner to elicit a response allows you the teacher to assess the learner's knowledge, while allowing the learner to discover and understand what they are doing wrong, why and how to improve the driving task. Any practical demonstration of technique must be clear and suitable. The learner should be kept fully involved and given the opportunity to explore their understanding of what they are being shown.

Competence is demonstrated where a trainer:

- Checks understanding and is prepared to repeat an explanation.

- Gives clear, timely, and technically accurate explanations or demonstrations.

- Finds a different way to demonstrate or explain if the learner still does not understand.

Feedback

Learners need to have a clear picture of how they are performing against their learning objectives. This should be reinforced throughout the lesson. Feedback needs to be appropriate and timely. This can take the form of encouragement when they are performing well, coaching where they need help, or as a further learning opportunity. However, a constant flow of words, however technically accurate, given at an unsuitable time, may be de-motivating or actually dangerous. Sitting quietly and saying nothing can also be an immensely powerful form of feedback in some situations. Remember the key words here—appropriate and timely.

Feedback should be balanced with the positive and negative; it also needs to be relevant and honest. It is not helpful if the learner is given unrealistic feedback that creates a false sense of their own ability. If a learner needs to be told that something is wrong or dangerous, there is no point in waffling. The learner should have a realistic and clear sense of their own performance.

Always remember that feedback is a two-way process. Ideally, it should be prompted by the learner, with the trainer responding to the learner's questions or comments. The learner's feedback should never be overlooked or disregarded.

Competence is demonstrated where a trainer:

- Provides feedback in response to questions from the learner.

- Seeks appropriate opportunities to provide feedback that reinforces understanding or confirms achievement of learning objectives.

- Provides feedback about failure to achieve learning objectives, to help the learner achieve an understanding of what they need to do to improve.

- Provides feedback that the learner can understand.

- Provides consistent feedback that is reinforced by body language.

Learner's queries

Direct questions or queries from the learner need to be dealt with as soon as possible. The response may involve providing information or directing the learner to a suitable reference source. Trainers should encourage learners to discover answers for themselves. Learners may not always have the confidence to ask direct questions, and so the ADI should be able to pick up comments or non-verbal communication, such as body language or facial expressions, that indicate uncertainty or confusion. Use this as an opportunity to explore any possible issues.

Competence is demonstrated where a trainer:

- Responds openly and readily to queries.

- Provides helpful answers or directs the learner to suitable sources of information.

- Actively checks with learner, if their comments or body language suggest they may have a question.

- Encourages the learner to explore possible solutions for themselves.

Professional approach

Learners should feel comfortable expressing their own opinions. Trainers should create an open, friendly environment for learning, regardless of the learner's age, gender, sexual orientation, ethnic background, religion, physical abilities, or any other irrelevant factor. This implies active respect for the learner, their values, and what constitutes appropriate behaviour in their culture.

The ADI must not display inappropriate attitudes or behaviours towards other road users and should challenge their learner if they display these behaviours. Competence is demonstrated where a trainer:

- Keeps a respectful distance, not invading the learner's personal space.

- Asks the learner how they wish to be addressed.

- Asks a disabled driver to explain their condition and what their needs are.

- Adopts an appropriate position in the car.

- Uses language about other road users that is not derogatory and does not invite the learner to collude with any discriminatory attitude or behaviours.

End of session performance review

Learners should be encouraged to reflect on their own performance and discuss their feelings with the trainer. The ADI should encourage honest self-appraisal and use client-centred techniques to highlight areas that need development if the learner has not recognised them. Once development areas have been identified, the learner should be encouraged to make them part of their future development.

Your Standards Check assessment result will be graded simply "A" or "B":

- Grade A: An overall high standard of competence

- Grade B: A sufficient level of competence.

An unsatisfactory performance is simply a "fail".

The effectiveness of the trainer's lesson delivery is scored by the examiner. A score of 85% or over will achieve an "A" Grade; below 60% is a fail. Anything in between is a satisfactory standard and graded with a "B".

Formal details of the three main or "high" areas of competence areas: "Lesson Planning", "Risk Management," and "Teaching and Learning Strategies" are given on the Standards Check form SC1 (Appendix 6). When assessing the trainer's ability, points are awarded to each of seventeen sub-competencies (sometimes called "lower" level competence).

Points are allocated according to performance shown:

- No evidence of competence = 0

- A few elements of competence demonstrated = 1

- Competence demonstrated in most elements = 2

- Competence demonstrated in all elements = 3

As well as achieving a minimum of 31 points out of 51 to pass, a minimum score of 8 in the Risk Management area is also necessary. The minimum score for an "A" grade is 43.

This marking scheme provides the trainer with a written profile of strong areas, and of weak areas where development is needed. The grade awarded is calculated on how well the trainer meets the learner's training needs. ADIs are expected to consider using a Client-Centred Learning approach, where an onus is put on the learner to share responsibility for recognising the driving risks during the lesson. This involves not only encouraging the learner to talk about their goals, feelings, and concerns, but also actively listening to what the learner has to say. It is important to recognise other indications, e.g. body language and/or facial expressions, where the learner is trying to express something but perhaps cannot find the right words.

Finally, the Standards Check grade will continue to determine the period before the next assessment check. Realistically, at present, the grade awarded has more meaning inside the industry than with customers. For instance, where a school is recruiting ADIs, the grade is likely to be of interest, and some insurers may also offer a discount for the top grade. An instructor trainer would be expected to be Grade A in order to maintain credibility. However, when marketing to the public, a friendly demeanour and a reputation for punctuality and reliability are more likely to create new business than touting the "A" grade on the Standards Check. Regardless though, being a "Grade A instructor" certainly will not do you any harm and can only back up your claims of professional ability with an official stamp.

A further note: although an ADI may be industry-qualified to teach emergency response driving, the DVSA will not allow this type of lesson to be conducted on a Standards Check for health and safety reasons. The "learner" will be required to comply with red traffic signals and traffic signs. The same rule applies to off-road training, such as four-wheel drive on rough terrain and skid-control events. The lesson being assessed must be a "normal" type of driving lesson.

To stay up to date with the views on the Standards Check, tips on improving your grade, and to hear the different opinions from other ADIs, join one or more of the industry trade associations. You will find their contact details in this book.

A bit more about the Standards Check
While the learner is usually a provisional licence holder, it can be a qualified driver having a refresher or advanced driving lesson (but not another ADI). You must bring your ADI licence, and your car needs to meet the minimum test vehicle requirements.

The Standards Check is conducted by a specially trained examiner who observes and assesses a one-hour live driving lesson. The examiner is trained to focus on recognising achievement and the promoting of improvement and development—rather than purely identifying driving faults.

The ADI's task is ultimately to provide an effective learning experience. This is judged to be one in which the learner is supported to take as much responsibility as possible for their own learning.

FREQUENCY OF THE STANDARDS CHECK

The DVSA uses ADI pass rates to prioritise when ADIs will receive a Standards Check. Four indicators are considered. If three of them are triggered, then the trainer is likely to be called for a check. The indicators are:

1. Average number of driving faults per test (five or more).

2. Average number of serious faults per test (0.5 or more).

3. Percentage of tests where the driving examiner had to take physical action in the interests of public safety (10% or higher).

4. Overall pass rate over the rolling 12 months (55% or lower).

The indicators will only be used if the trainer brings five or more learners for driving tests in a 12-month period. Where a trainer brings fewer than five learners, or the trainer does not teach learners, the Standards Check will take place once every four years.

Before the Standards Check is conducted, the examiner will contact the trainer to arrange an "engagement call" for 30 minutes. In that time, the discussion will be about:

- The ADI driver test analysis report.

- Where further support and guidance can be gained.

- What will happen when taking the Standards Check.

As always, we advise trainers to join a Trade Association. Make sure you get advice and guidance before the DVSA make contact, so that you are prepared.

CHAPTER 9

HOW TO PLAN A DRIVING LESSON

Be organised

DRIVING LESSON PLANS

A goal without a plan is just a wish.

The minimum lesson plan must agree with each learner about what needs to be achieved during the period of training. Then, at the end of the session, an evaluation needs to be made of how much was accomplished and what needs to be done next. When it comes to managing the content of the driving lesson, being in a relaxed mood is important; new learning cannot be achieved if the learner is a stressed state.

LESSON STRUCTURE

Driving lessons always need to be planned. Each learner almost always knows something about the task at hand, so you need to establish what this is. They will have pedestrian skills, possibly cycling skills, or may even have driven before. Virtually everyone has been a passenger in a vehicle. So, use their knowledge to start building their learning plan, teaching from the "known to the unknown", "simple to the complex" and "observation to reasoning".

Every driving lesson needs to have a start, middle, and an end. The usual structure includes:

- Check/recap briefly on any relevant previous training.

- Determine learner's knowledge and experience to establish the learner's stage of ability—Identify Training Needs (ITN).

- Gain agreement with the learner about what will be the core topic of the lesson.

- Determine a suitable route or training area.

- Consider the typical driving faults to expect.

- Time management of the lesson.

- Finish the lesson on a high—focusing on a good point such as an achievement.

ROUTE PLANNING

Driving skills should be introduced in a logical order that suits the learner's ability, the geographic location, and the time of day when a lesson is taken, taking into consideration the prevailing road, traffic, and weather conditions.

The training route needs to be appropriate for the lesson topic. Be prepared to repeat any relevant parts of the same route. This will help ensure that learning is being achieved, especially before repeating the learning topic in a more challenging environment or situation; allowing learners to build their confidence and understanding.

LESSON PLAN PRESENTATION

We begin each plan with an outline of the key learning areas. These map the important subject areas for the lesson. From this starting point, the driver trainer needs to decide how much further detail is needed for the learner and the lesson to be delivered effectively.

It will be a matter for individual decision about when, where and how to introduce the higher levels of the Goals for Driver Education (GDE) matrix. The driver trainer decides here. Managing the needs of Client Centred Learning may sometimes be at odds with the GDE Matrix, but neither should affect the overall contribution and importance of each in the complete learning to drive process.

SKILLS DEVELOPMENT

Learning will be achieved by doing.

Practice does make perfect, and to facilitate this the trainer should plan the best way(s) to achieve learning. Consider using:

1. Clear, concise explanations, reviewing the relevant theory and accepted facts.

2. Simple, easy directions/satellite navigation.

3. Offering a practical demonstration.

4. Drawing or using illustrations.

5. Instruction/coaching suited to the learner's ability.

6. Prompts to enable solutions. These should be found by the learner, not by the trainer. Questioning is a good way to check topic knowledge and/or allow the learner driver to give feedback. Open questions (why, who, what, when...) are better than closed questions (yes or no).

7. Observing other road users, collecting information to develop system of driving and/or explore the higher levels of the GDE Matrix.

8. Feedback—to give positive reinforcement and encourage correct behaviour and/or to correct criticised behaviour.

9. Intervention, verbally or with the dual controls, to prevent a serious situation.

10. Learner self-assessment (GDE Matrix) to reflect on achievement.

11. Commentary driving.

POSITIVE FAULT CORRECTION

Yes, learners make mistakes, but they also do things well. Focusing on positive outcomes and people's strengths, being honest but not criticising the person, helps. Try these three questions:

1. What went well?

2. What did not go so well?

3. What could you improve upon next time?

IDENTIFY TRAINING NEEDS (ITN)

When judging the level of a learner's ability, you will need to customise the lesson plan(s) you wish to use. The "summary on a page" (SOAP) style plans in this book are generic and most of them can be adapted to the varying levels of driving ability. These are:

1. Inexperienced learners: An untrained beginner.

2. Partly Trained: Intermediate stage.

3. Fully Trained: About ready to take their practical driving test.

4. New full licence holder: Newly qualified driver, with little or no experience.

5. Experienced full licence holder: Fully qualified and experienced motorist.

If you have little or no experience of working with the learner, it may be that you need to identify training needs with a short assessment drive before finalising the lesson plan. It is impossible to structure the lesson correctly without agreeing learning goals and needs. Remember to be prepared to adapt your lesson plan to developing situations or the learner's needs as these arise.

LESSON PLAN INDEX

This index has three sections covering provisional licence holders as well as two main types of qualified driver. When using these plans, use and judge any input you need from the DVSA's national standard for "Safe and Responsible Driving (Category B)". The variations include use of manual and automatic vehicles; class of road; time; weather conditions; number of passengers; load; private and or commercial vehicle usage.

Five roles are identified. These can be read as units or modules:

1. Prepare vehicle and its occupants for a journey.

2. Guide and control the vehicle.

3. Use the road in accordance with the Highway Code.

4. Drive safely and responsibly in the traffic system.

5. Review and adjust driving behaviour over lifetime.

A. Lessons for the learner driver

i.   Explanation of the Controls

ii.   Moving Away and Making Normal Stops

iii.   Use of Mirrors

iv.   Use of Signals

v.   Emergency Stop

vi.   Approaching Junctions: Major to Minor

vii.   Approaching Junctions: Minor to Major

viii.   Crossroads

ix.   Roundabouts

x.   Pedestrian Crossings

xi.   Awareness and Anticipation

xii.   Judgement when Meeting & Crossing Approaching Traffic; Overtaking

xiii.   Keep Space: Clearances & Following Distances

xiv.   Use of Speed & Making Progress

xv.   Road Positioning

xvi.   Eco-Safe Driving

xvii.   Independent Driving

xviii. Traffic Signs, Signals and Road Markings

xix.   Satellite Navigation

xx.   Reversing

xxi.   Bay Parking

You should use your own professional judgement to decide the order in which you teach these subjects and topics. Always consider your learner's ability, as well as local circumstances. A reasonable degree of proficiency driving forwards is needed before attempting to teach manoeuvres that include reversing. Begin teaching the simpler things before moving on to those that are more complex.

B. Sessions for the newly qualified driver

The "Pass Plus" Course:

i.   Town Driving

ii. All Weather Driving

iii. Out of Town Driving and Rural Roads

iv. Night Driving

v.   Dual Carriageway Driving

vi. Motorway Driving

C. Sessions for the experienced qualified driver

- The Advanced Driving Course
- Corporate Driver Development

D. Additional license acquisition

- Car Towing
- Large Goods Vehicle
- Passenger Carrying Vehicle

You can adapt the advanced and corporate session plans to suit other courses for experienced qualified drivers, such as the National Driver Offender Retraining Scheme (NDORS) and Specialist Vehicle Type Training. Training providers will probably have their own course syllabus and guidance notes.

LESSON DIAGRAMS

A picture speaks a thousand words. Pre-drawn or self-drawn illustrations will make both teaching and learning easier. We have placed some diagrams alongside the relevant lesson content to help you.

You might also wish to use other excellent illustrations such as those in the "Highway Code" and publications such as *Driving: The Essential Skills*, or for advanced/corporate driver training, those in *Roadcraft*.

Lesson 1: Explanation of the Controls

Introducing Key Learning Areas

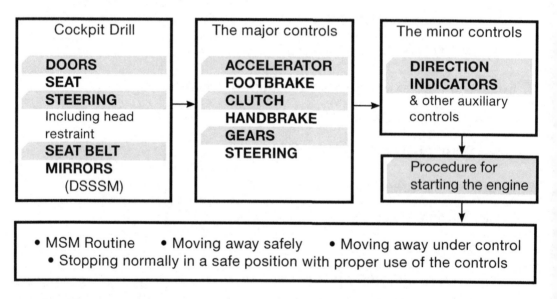

Cockpit Drill	The major controls	The minor controls
DOORS	**ACCELERATOR**	**DIRECTION**
SEAT	**FOOTBRAKE**	**INDICATORS**
STEERING	**CLUTCH**	& other auxiliary
Including head	**HANDBRAKE**	controls
restraint	**GEARS**	
SEAT BELT	**STEERING**	
MIRRORS		Procedure for
(DSSSM)		starting the engine

- MSM Routine   • Moving away safely   • Moving away under control
  • Stopping normally in a safe position with proper use of the controls

Preparation Notes:

This would normally be a lesson for a complete beginner. Aim to cover the essential information within 45 minutes to allow a little time to attempt moving and stopping the car. Ideally this lesson should have a longer duration than one hour.

Essentials:

- Clutch diagram

- Parking and leaving the vehicle
  Use your left hand to open your driver's door

Location:

Nursey patch. Quiet flat road

Goals for Driver Education (GDE) matrix

Level 1

National standard for driving cars and light vans:

Role 1 Preparing the vehicle for a journey

Role 2: Guide and control the vehicle

Anything else?

You decide ...

I really struggle with this	I need to be better at this	I am okay at this	I am pretty good at this	This is a real strength of mine
1	2	3	4	5

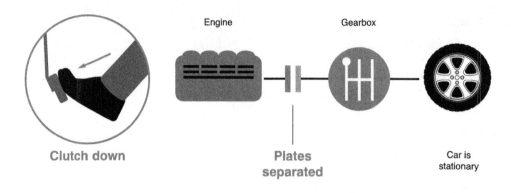

Engine

Gearbox

Clutch down

Plates separated

Car is stationary

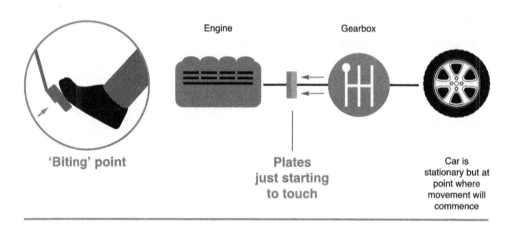

Engine

Gearbox

'Biting' point

Plates just starting to touch

Car is stationary but at point where movement will commence

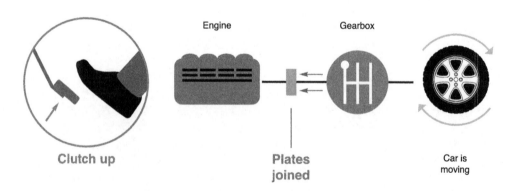

Engine

Gearbox

Clutch up

Plates joined

Car is moving

Lesson 2: Moving Away & Making Normal Stops

Introducing Key Learning Areas

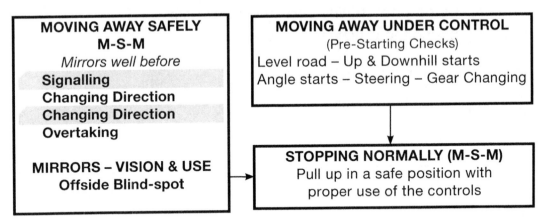

| MOVING AWAY SAFELY
M-S-M
Mirrors well before
Signalling
Changing Direction
Changing Direction
Overtaking

MIRRORS – VISION & USE
Offside Blind-spot | MOVING AWAY UNDER CONTROL
(Pre-Starting Checks)
Level road – Up & Downhill starts
Angle starts – Steering – Gear Changing

STOPPING NORMALLY (M-S-M)
Pull up in a safe position with
proper use of the controls |

Preparation Notes:

Moving the car off for the very first time is one of the most exciting and memorable moments for the new learner driver.

Talking your learner through the safe routine for moving away and stopping will usually require comprehensive guidance, known as 'full instruction'.

Guidance must be clear, accurate and concise, with sufficient detail to enable your learner to carry out the exercise successfully. The words you use are important, as is the timing of this instruction.

Essentials:

- Clutch diagram

- Dry run (Dummy run / Dress rehearsal)

- Dealing with a stalled engine

- Use "Preparation – Observation – Manoeuvre" (POM) Routine

Location:

Nursey patch. Quiet flat road

Goals for Driver Education (GDE) matrix

Level 1

National standard for driving cars and light vans:

Role 1 Preparing the vehicle for a journey

Role 2: Guide and control the vehicle:

Anything else?

You decide ...

I really struggle with this	I need to be better at this	I am okay at this	I am pretty good at this	This is a real strength of mine
1	2	3	4	5

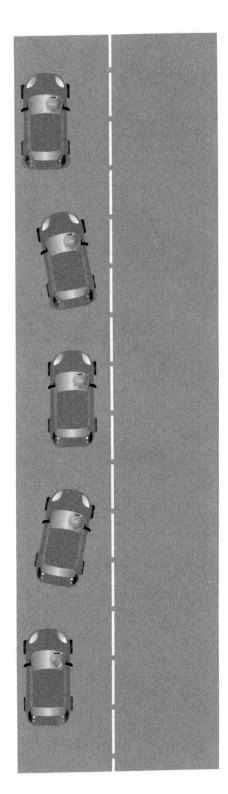

Lesson 3: Use of Mirrors

Introducing Key Learning Areas

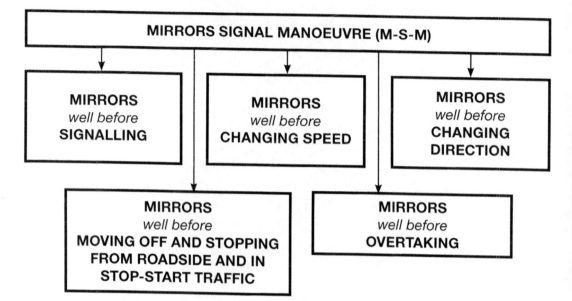

Preparation Notes:

Good forward planning and anticipation includes seeing what is following or at the side of the car. Dealing with closely following traffic and potential third-party aggressive behaviour.

Essentials:

- No head movement for checking interior mirror
- Some head movement for checking exterior mirrors
- Hierarchy of road users (pedal cyclists)

Location:

Suited to learner's ability and competence

Goals for Driver Education (GDE) matrix

Level 2, 3 & 4

National standard for driving cars and light vans:

Role 2: Guide and control the vehicle

Role 3: Use the road in accordance with the Highway Code

Role 4: Drive safely and responsibly in the traffic system

Anything else?

You decide ...

I really struggle with this	I need to be better at this	I am okay at this	I am pretty good at this	This is a real strength of mine
1	2	3	4	5

Lesson 4: Use of Signals

Introducing Key Learning Areas

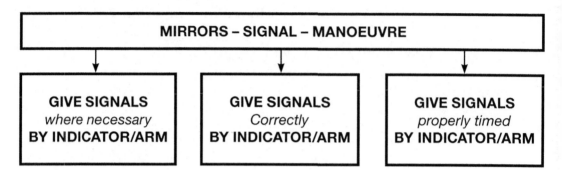

MIRRORS – SIGNAL – MANOEUVRE

GIVE SIGNALS *where necessary* **BY INDICATOR/ARM**	**GIVE SIGNALS** *Correctly* **BY INDICATOR/ARM**	**GIVE SIGNALS** *properly timed* **BY INDICATOR/ARM**

Preparation Notes:

Signals are the most obvious means of communication between drivers and all other road users. It is important that direction signals are given correctly, in a clear and unmistakable manner. Arms signals for drivers and riders are still shown in the Highway Code. We can expect arm signals to be used by pedal cyclists and horse riders.

Drivers complain about the lack of signals from other drivers. To overcome this, we can identify how a driver's intention may be determined by where he or she is looking, the vehicles speed, or the direction where the vehicle's front wheels are pointing. An example of this is when dealing with roundabout approach.

Essentials:

- "Mirrors – Signal – Manoeuvre" Is given as advice in the Highway Code. Signals do need to be given where they would benefit another road user.

Location:

Suited to learner's ability and competence

Goals for Driver Education (GDE) matrix

Level 2

National standard for driving cars and light vans:

Role 2: Guide and control the vehicle

Role 3: Use the road in accordance with the Highway Code

Role 4: Drive safely and responsibly in the traffic system

Anything else?

You decide …

I really struggle with this	I need to be better at this	I am okay at this	I am pretty good at this	This is a real strength of mine
1	2	3	4	5

Lesson 5: Emergency Stop

Introducing Key Learning Areas

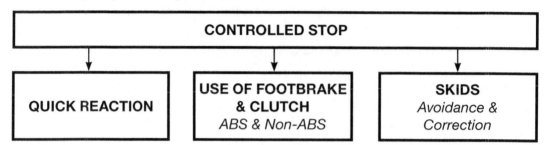

Preparation Notes:

Having instructed an untrained learner to move off and make a normal stop, you need to decide on which lesson to introduce the emergency stop exercise.

Where a learner is also taking private practice, probably be in a car without dual controls, you should introduce this exercise earlier rather than on later lessons.

Essentials:

- With good anticipation there should seldom be a need for any driver to have to perform an emergency stop as opposed to a normal stop.

Location:

Quiet road with no following traffic

Goals for Driver Education (GDE) matrix

Level 1

National standard for driving cars and light vans:

Role 2: Guide and control the vehicle

Anything else?

You decide ...

I really struggle with this	I need to be better at this	I am okay at this	I am pretty good at this	This is a real strength of mine
1	2	3	4	5

Lesson 6: Approaching Junctions – Major to Minor

Introducing Key Learning Areas

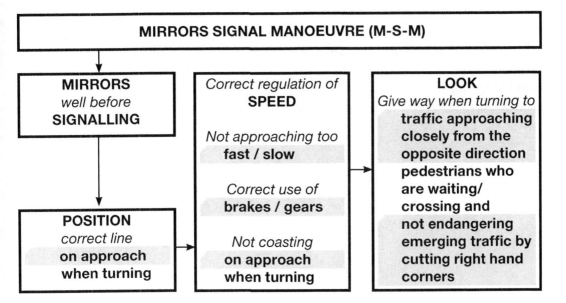

MIRRORS SIGNAL MANOEUVRE (M-S-M)

MIRRORS well before **SIGNALLING**	*Correct regulation of* **SPEED**	**LOOK** *Give way when turning to* **traffic approaching closely from the opposite direction pedestrians who are waiting/ crossing and not endangering emerging traffic by cutting right hand corners**
POSITION *correct line* **on approach when turning**	*Not approaching too* **fast / slow** *Correct use of* **brakes / gears** *Not coasting* **on approach when turning**	

Preparation Notes:

Most collisions will occur at junctions because this is where all types of traffic meet. This is an opportunity to review third party behaviour, including not only drivers, but those on two wheels, including electric scooters.

Essentials:

- Use "Mirrors – Signal – Manoeuvre" routine as shown above.

- Hierarchy of road users

Location:

Quiet residential roads to begin with.

Goals for Driver Education (GDE) matrix

Level 2, 3 & 4

National standard for driving cars and light vans:

Role 2: Guide and control the vehicle

Role 3: Use the road in accordance with the Highway Code

Role 4: Drive safely and responsibly in the traffic system

Anything else?

You decide …

I really struggle with this	I need to be better at this	I am okay at this	I am pretty good at this	This is a real strength of mine
1	2	3	4	5

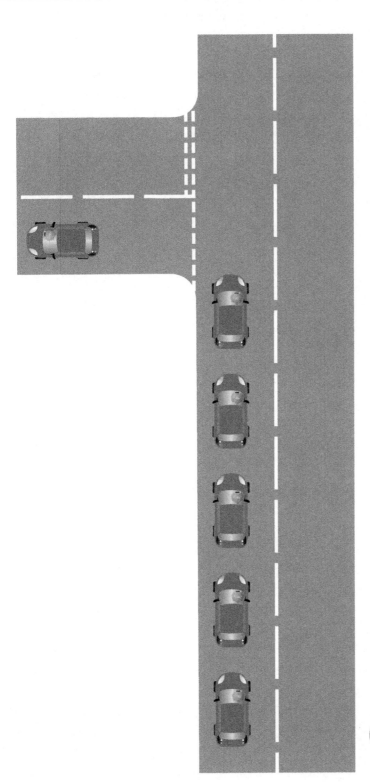

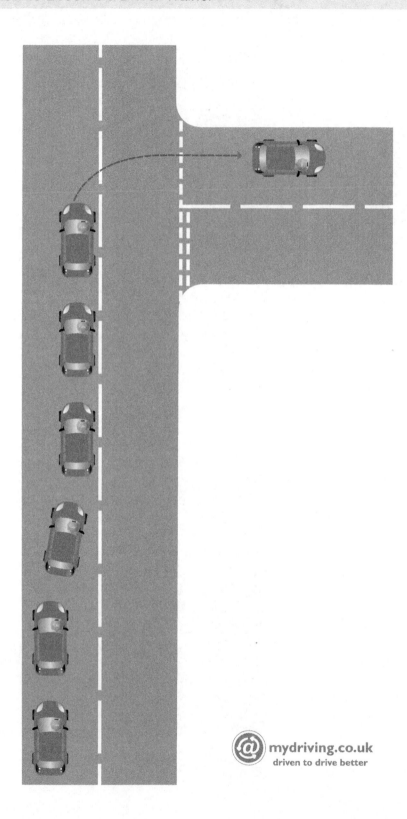

Lesson 7: Approaching Junctions – Minor to Major

Introducing Key Learning Areas

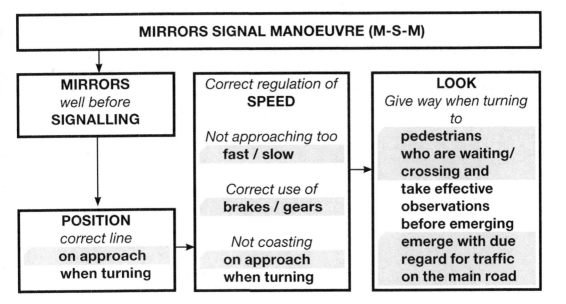

MIRRORS SIGNAL MANOEUVRE (M-S-M)

MIRRORS well before **SIGNALLING**	*Correct regulation of* **SPEED**	**LOOK** *Give way when turning to*
	Not approaching too **fast / slow**	**pedestrians who are waiting/ crossing and** take effective observations
POSITION *correct line* **on approach when turning**	*Correct use of* **brakes / gears**	before emerging **emerge with due regard for traffic on the main road**
	Not coasting **on approach when turning**	

Preparation Notes:

Most collisions will occur at junctions because this is where all types of traffic meet. This is an opportunity to review third party behaviour, including not only drivers, but those on two wheels, including electric scooters.

Essentials:

- Use "Mirrors – Signal – Manoeuvre" routine as shown above.

- Hierarchy of road users

Location:

Quiet residential roads to begin with.

Goals for Driver Education (GDE) matrix

Level 2, 3 & 4

National standard for driving cars and light vans:

Role 2: Guide and control the vehicle

Role 3: Use the road in accordance with the Highway Code

Role 4: Drive safely and responsibly in the traffic system

Anything else?

You decide …

I really struggle with this	I need to be better at this	I am okay at this	I am pretty good at this	This is a real strength of mine
1	2	3	4	5

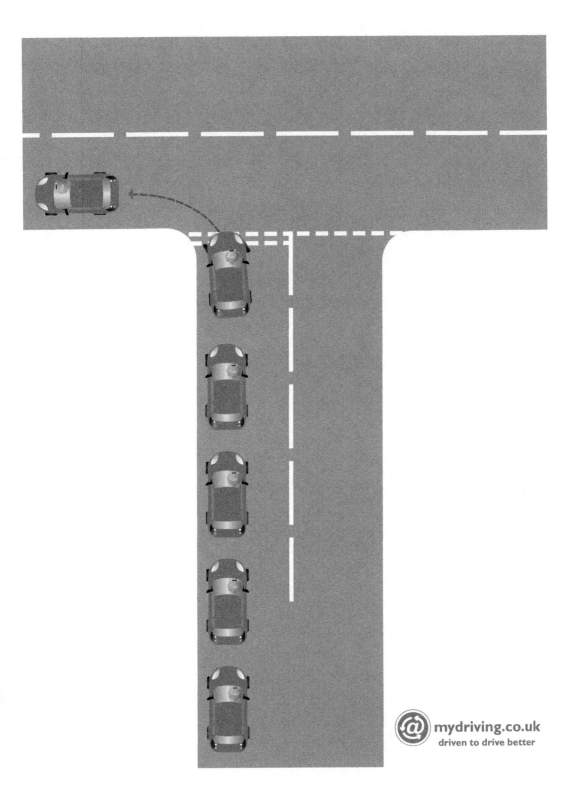

mydriving.co.uk
driven to drive better

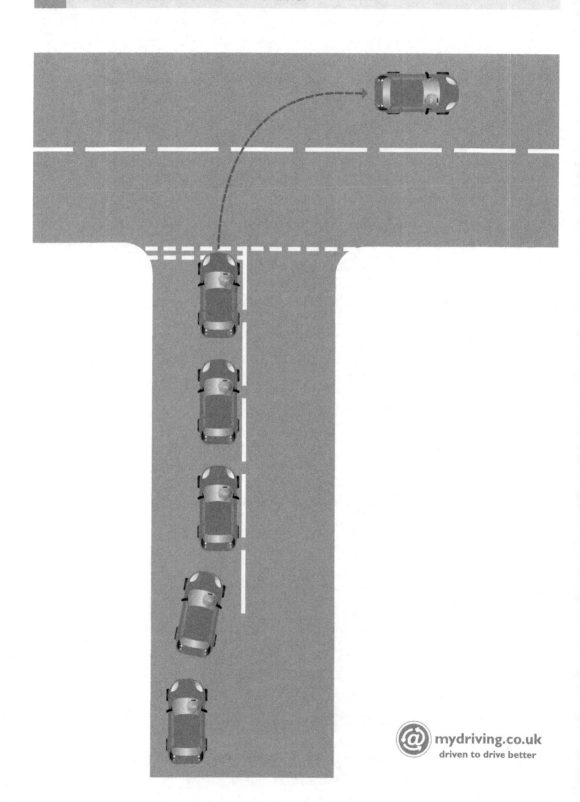

Lesson 8: Crossroads

Introducing Key Learning Areas

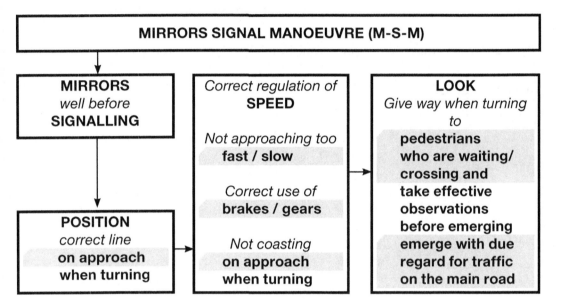

Preparation Notes:

Most collisions will occur at junctions because this is where all types of traffic meet. This is an opportunity to review other driver behaviour.

Essentials:

- Use "Mirrors – Signal – Manoeuvre" routine as shown above.

- Hierarchy of road users

Location:

Quiet residential roads to begin with.

Goals for Driver Education (GDE) matrix

Level 2, 3 & 4

National standard for driving cars and light vans:

Role 2: Guide and control the vehicle

Role 3: Use the road in accordance with the Highway Code

Role 4: Drive safely and responsibly in the traffic system

Anything else?

You decide ...

I really struggle with this	I need to be better at this	I am okay at this	I am pretty good at this	This is a real strength of mine
1	2	3	4	5

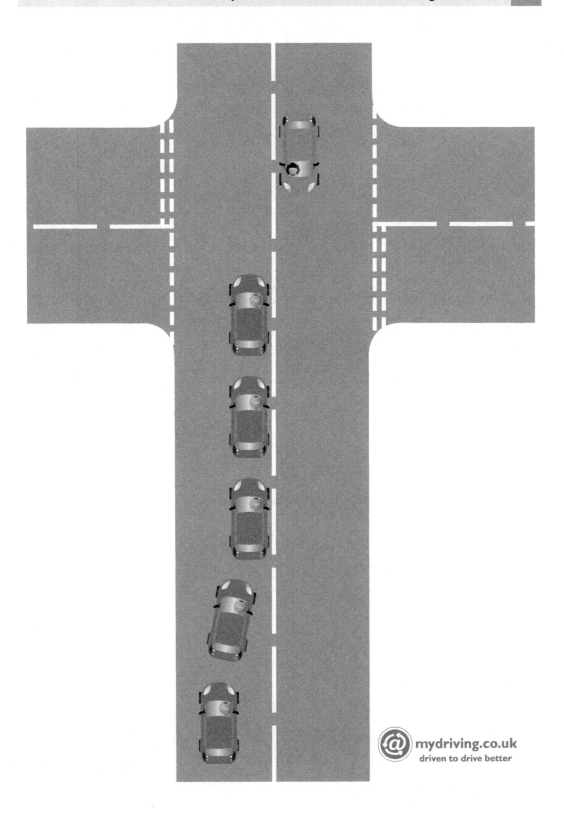

mydriving.co.uk
driven to drive better

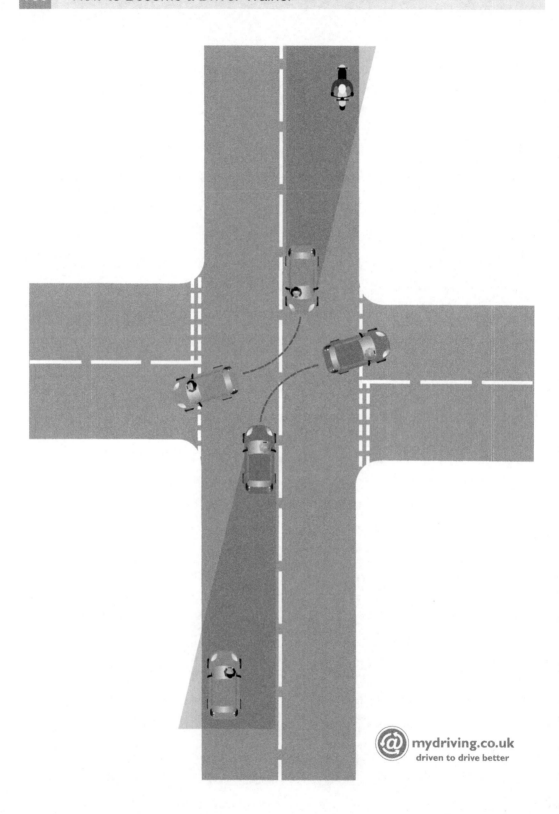

mydriving.co.uk
driven to drive better

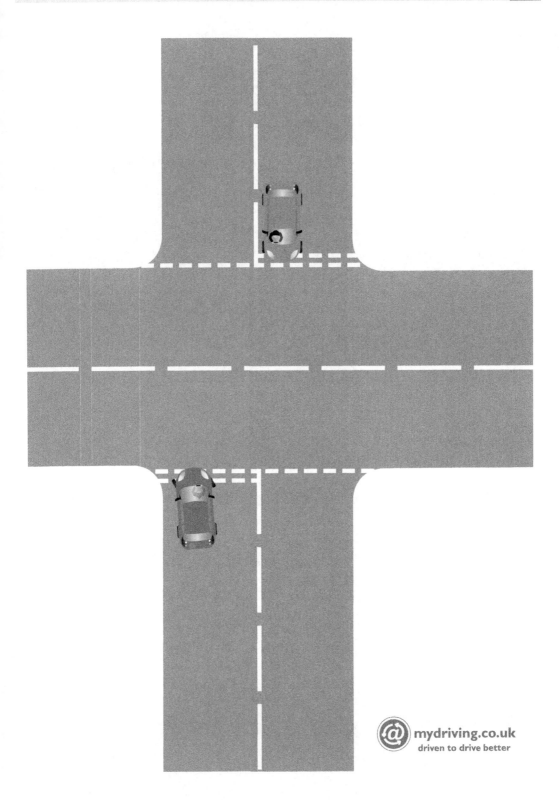

mydriving.co.uk
driven to drive better

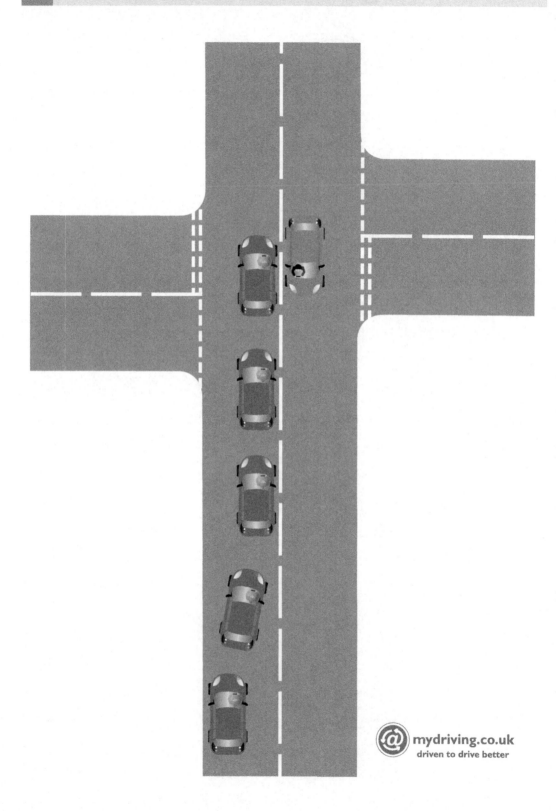

mydriving.co.uk
driven to drive better

Lesson 9: Roundabouts

Introducing Key Learning Areas

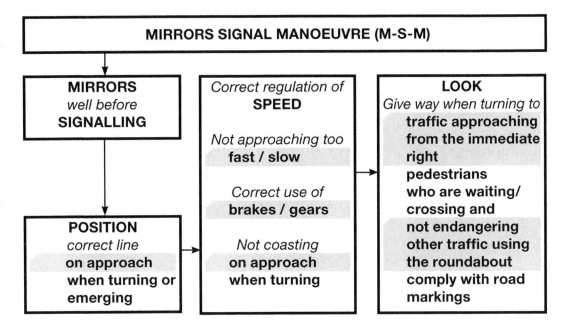

Preparation Notes:

Most collisions will occur at junctions, including roundabouts where rear-end shunts can be common. On approach learners must check for waiting traffic ahead, as well as looking for traffic with priority to the right. Review other driver behaviour and the need for lane discipline, particularly on large or complex roundabouts.

Introduce topic using a diagram to show the correct route through the roundabout to the chosen exit.

Essentials:

- Use "Mirrors – Signal – Manoeuvre" routine as shown above.

- Hierarchy of road users

Location:

Quiet residential roads to begin with.

Goals for Driver Education (GDE) matrix

Level 2, 3 & 4

National standard for driving cars and light vans:

Role 2: Guide and control the vehicle

Role 3: Use the road in accordance with the Highway Code

Role 4: Drive safely and responsibly in the traffic system

Anything else?

You decide …

I really struggle with this	I need to be better at this	I am okay at this	I am pretty good at this	This is a real strength of mine
1	2	3	4	5

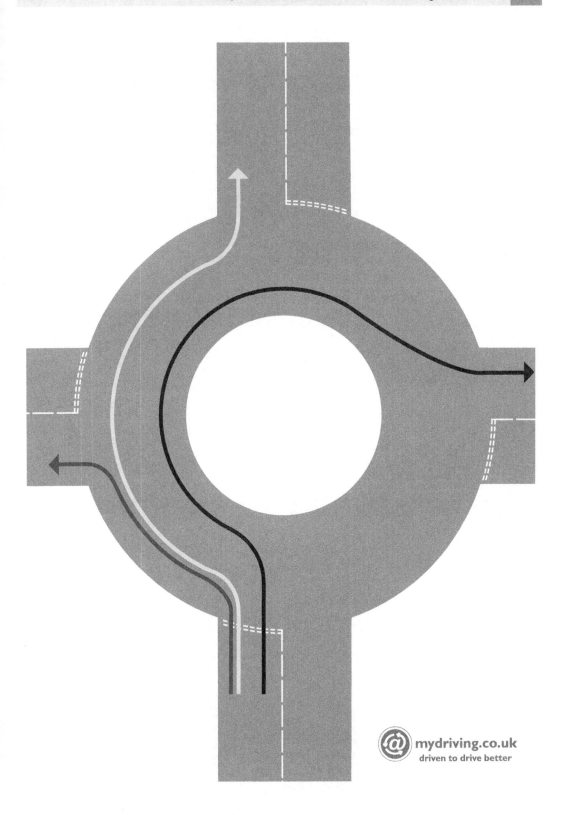

mydriving.co.uk
driven to drive better

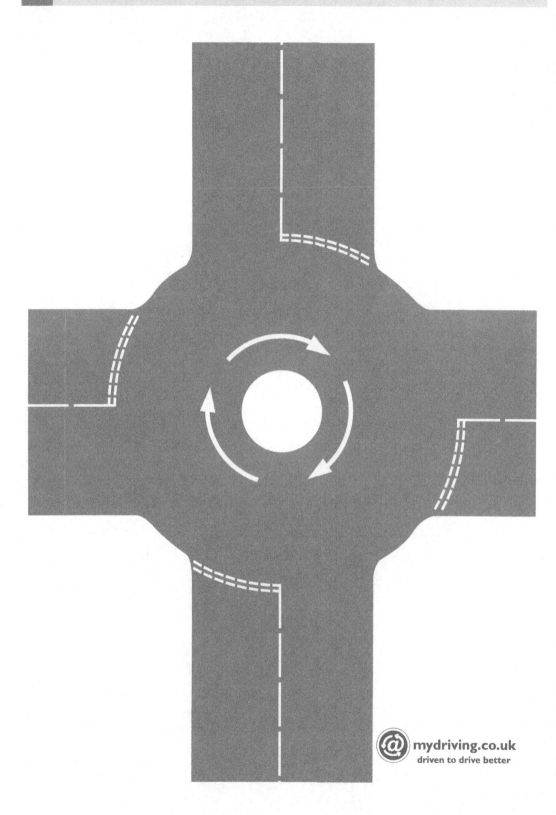

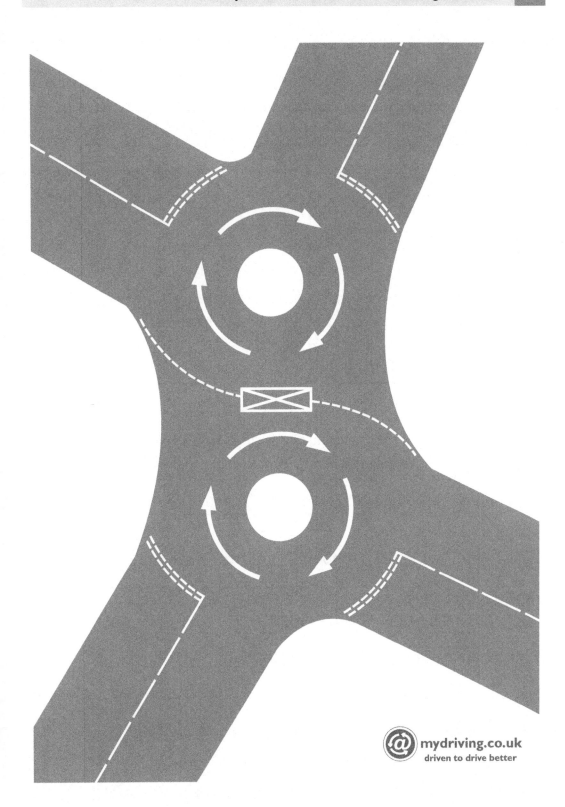

mydriving.co.uk
driven to drive better

Lesson 10: Pedestrian Crossings

Introducing Key Learning Areas

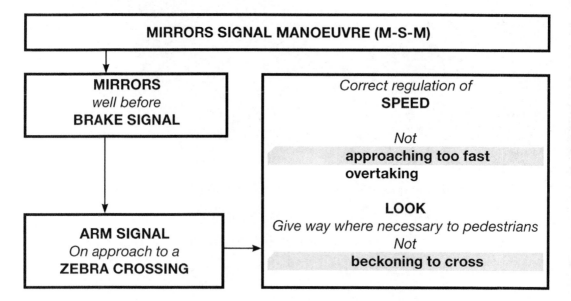

Preparation Notes:

Cover all types of both controlled and non-controlled pedestrian crossings, including parallel crossings. This is an opportunity to review pedestrian expectations and behaviour where there are refuges in the centre of the road.

Essentials:

Adapt "Mirrors – Signal – Manoeuvre" routine as shown above.

Location:

Usually, the High Street or similar road.

Goals for Driver Education (GDE) matrix

Level 2, 3 & 4

National standard for driving cars and light vans:

Role 2: Guide and control the vehicle

Role 3: Use the road in accordance with the Highway Code

Role 4: Drive safely and responsibly in the traffic system

Anything else?

You decide ...

I really struggle with this	I need to be better at this	I am okay at this	I am pretty good at this	This is a real strength of mine
1	2	3	4	5

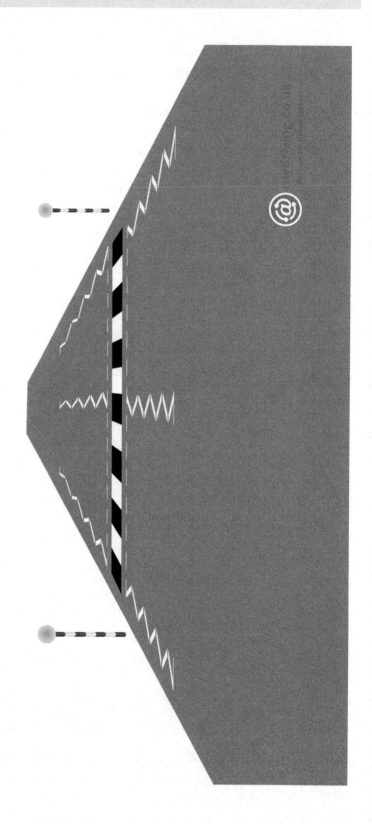

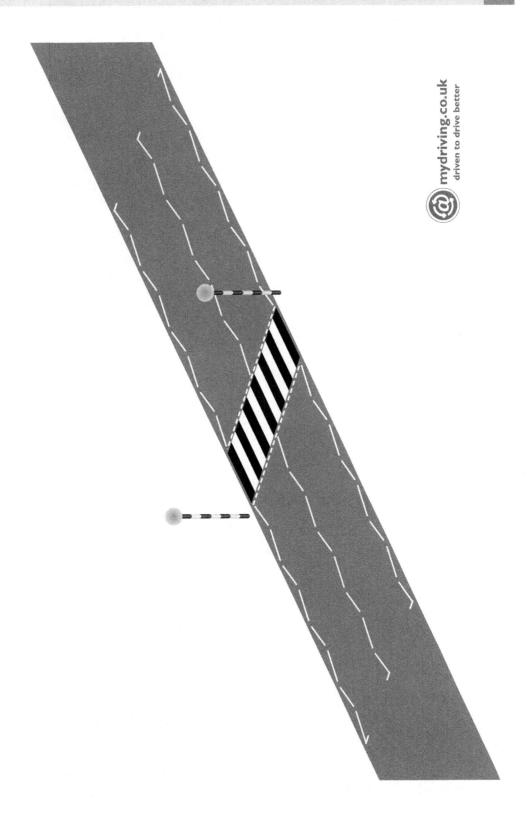

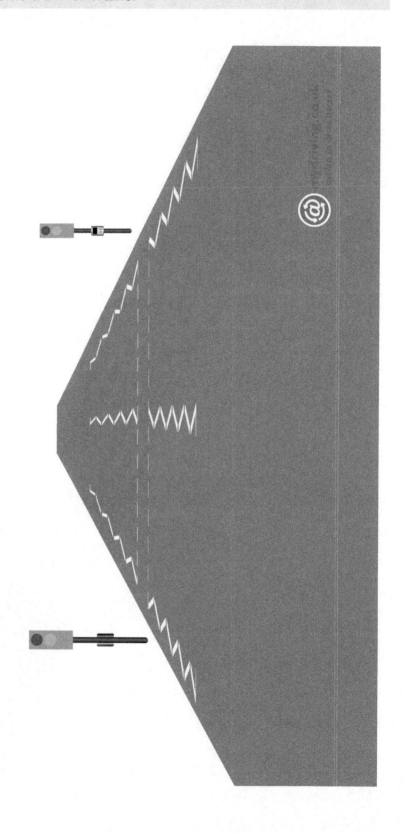

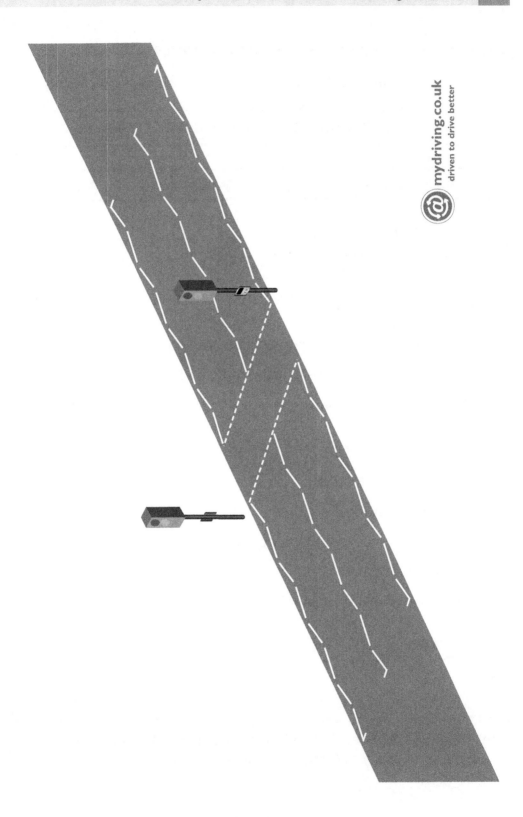

Lesson 11: Awareness and Anticipation (What if?)

Introducing Key Learning Areas

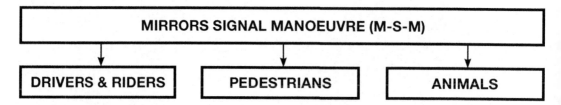

Preparation Notes:
- **Hierarchy of all road users**
  Highway Code revisions

Judgment approaching road hazards ...

1. Fixed features such as road junctions or bends

2. Moving features such as vehicle traffic and pedestrians

3. Changing weather conditions

Good forward planning and anticipation.

a. What can be seen ahead?

b. What cannot be seen?

c. What might you expect to happen?

d. Prioritise hazards

e. What to do if things change?

Driving styles, consideration for other road users and coping with incidents of aggressive behaviour.

Essentials:
Apply "Mirrors – Signal – Manoeuvre" routine to individual circumstances with good anticipation. Pedestrians stepping out from behind buses at stops is one of many "What if" examples.

Location:
All roads.

Goals for Driver Education (GDE) matrix
Level 2, 3 & 4

National standard for driving cars and light vans:
Role 2: Guide and control the vehicle

Role 3: Use the road in accordance with the Highway Code

Role 4: Drive safely and responsibly in the traffic system

Anything else?
You decide …

I really struggle with this	I need to be better at this	I am okay at this	I am pretty good at this	This is a real strength of mine
1	2	3	4	5

Lesson 12: Judgement when Meeting & Crossing Approaching Traffic; Overtaking other Traffic

Introducing Key Learning Areas

MIRRORS SIGNAL MANOEUVRE (M-S-M)

MEETING	CROSSING	OVERTAKING
Approaching traffic safely	*Approaching traffic safely*	*traffic safely*

Preparation Notes:

Judgment approaching traffic situations …

1. When to wait

2. When to go

Driving styles, consideration for other road users and coping with incidents of aggressive behaviour.

Learners will overtake pedal cyclists and buses serving their stops – early anticipation using MSM routine.

Essentials:

Apply "Mirrors – Signal – Manoeuvre" routine to individual circumstances.

Location:

All roads.

Goals for Driver Education (GDE) matrix

Level 2, 3 & 4

National standard for driving cars and light vans:

Role 2: Guide and control the vehicle

Role 3: Use the road in accordance with the Highway Code

Role 4: Drive safely and responsibly in the traffic system

Anything else?

You decide ...

I really struggle with this	I need to be better at this	I am okay at this	I am pretty good at this	This is a real strength of mine
1	2	3	4	5

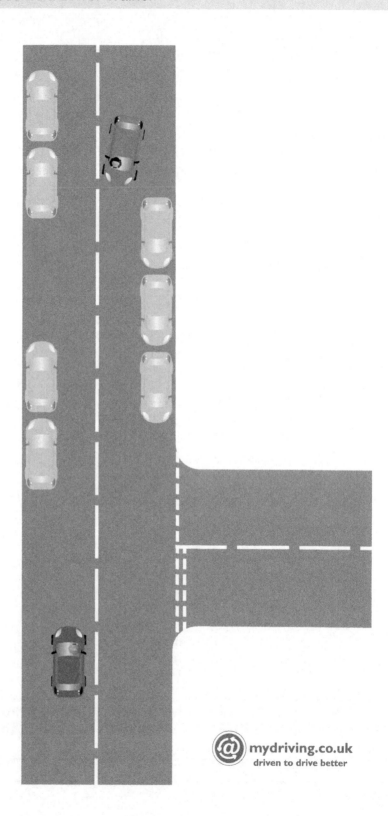

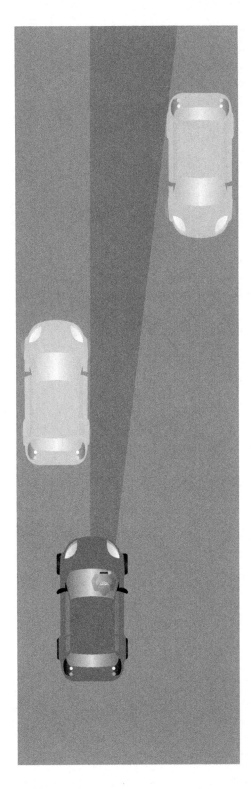

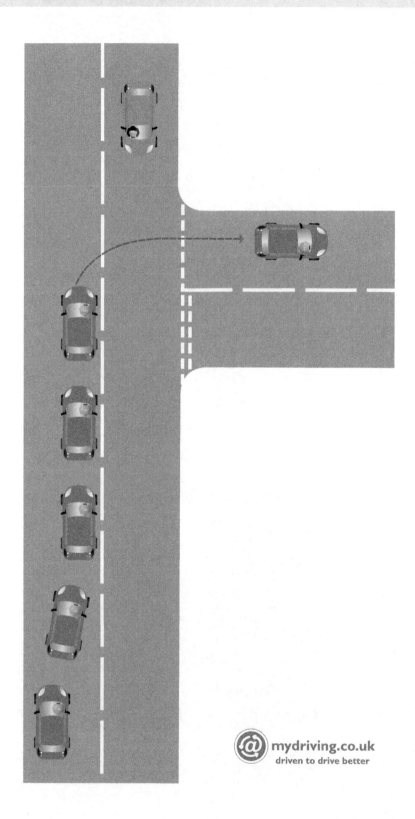

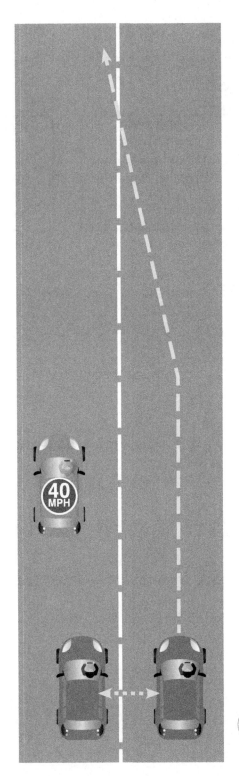

mydriving.co.uk
driven to drive better

Lesson 13: Keep Space - Clearances & Following Distances

Introducing Key Learning Areas

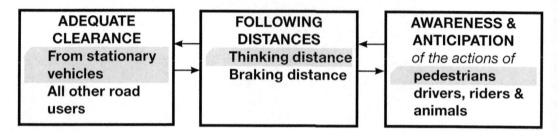

ADEQUATE CLEARANCE From stationary vehicles All other road users	FOLLOWING DISTANCES Thinking distance Braking distance	AWARENESS & ANTICIPATION *of the actions of* pedestrians drivers, riders & animals

Preparation Notes:

- **Hierarchy of all road users**
  Highway Code revisions

Judgment approaching traffic situations ... road position

1. Not too close to the left or approaching traffic

2. Not too close to vehicles in front

Driving styles, consideration for other road users and coping with incidents of aggressive behaviour.

Essentials:

Apply previous theory learning eg vehicle separation and stopping distances

Apply "Mirrors – Signal – Manoeuvre" routine to individual circumstances.

Location:

All roads.

Goals for Driver Education (GDE) matrix

Level 2, 3 & 4

National standard for driving cars and light vans:

Role 2: Guide and control the vehicle

Role 3: Use the road in accordance with the Highway Code

Role 4: Drive safely and responsibly in the traffic system

Anything else?

You decide ...

I really struggle with this	I need to be better at this	I am okay at this	I am pretty good at this	This is a real strength of mine
1	2	3	4	5

METRES

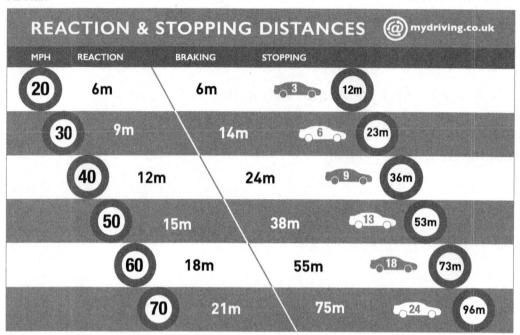

FEET

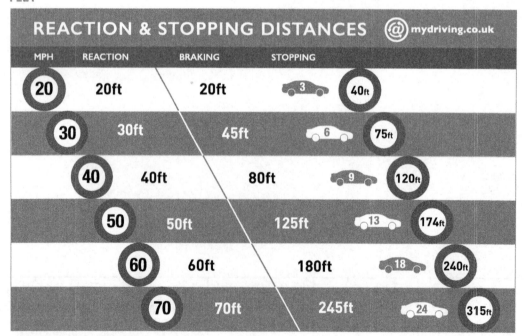

mydriving.co.uk
driven to drive better

Lesson 14: Use of Speed and Making Progress

Introducing Key Learning Areas

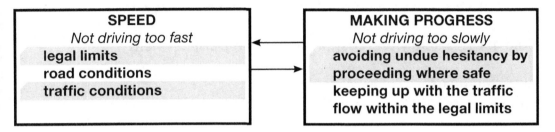

SPEED	MAKING PROGRESS
Not driving too fast	*Not driving too slowly*
legal limits **road conditions** **traffic conditions**	**avoiding undue hesitancy by** **proceeding where safe** **keeping up with the traffic** **flow within the legal limits**

Preparation Notes:
How to judge vehicle speed, including use of the speedometer

How to judge safe speed in varying traffic conditions circumstances

How to use visibility "limit points" on faster country roads

Driving styles, consideration for other road users and coping with incidents of aggressive behaviour.

Essentials:
Apply previous theory learning eg vehicle separation and stopping distances

"No speed limit is ever a target"

"Drive at a safe speed for the traffic and road conditions"

"Twenty is plenty"

"You can be driving too fast, even within the speed limit"

Location:
All roads.

Goals for Driver Education (GDE) matrix
Level 2, 3 & 4

National standard for driving cars and light vans:

Role 2: Guide and control the vehicle

Role 3: Use the road in accordance with the Highway Code

Role 4: Drive safely and responsibly in the traffic system

Anything else?

You decide ...

I really struggle with this	I need to be better at this	I am okay at this	I am pretty good at this	This is a real strength of mine
1	2	3	4	5

Lesson 15: Road Positioning and Lane Discipline

Introducing Key Learning Areas

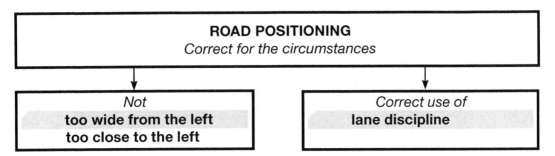

ROAD POSITIONING
Correct for the circumstances

| Not
too wide from the left
too close to the left | Correct use of
lane discipline |

Preparation Notes:
Applying the rule of the road when driving ahead …

1. on an empty, clear roads

2. where there are obstructions or traffic management schemes including bus lanes

Driving styles, consideration for other road users and coping with incidents of aggressive behaviour.

Essentials:
Apply "Mirrors – Signal – Manoeuvre" routine to individual circumstances.

Location:
All roads.

Goals for Driver Education (GDE) matrix
Level 2, 3 & 4

National standard for driving cars and light vans:
Role 2: Guide and control the vehicle

Role 3: Use the road in accordance with the Highway Code

Role 4: Drive safely and responsibly in the traffic system

Anything else?

You decide ...

I really struggle with this	I need to be better at this	I am okay at this	I am pretty good at this	This is a real strength of mine
1	2	3	4	5

Lesson 16: Eco-Safe Driving

Introducing Key Learning Areas

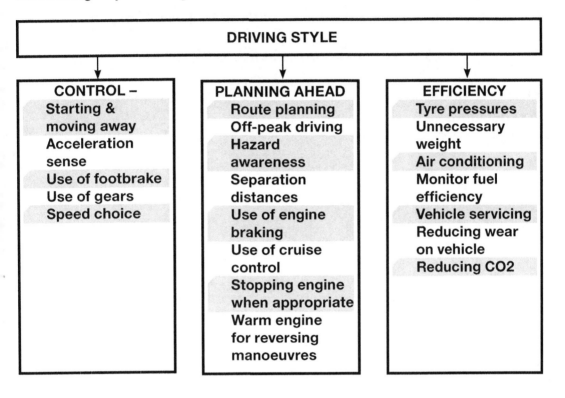

DRIVING STYLE		
CONTROL –	**PLANNING AHEAD**	**EFFICIENCY**
Starting & moving away	Route planning	Tyre pressures
Acceleration sense	Off-peak driving	Unnecessary weight
Use of footbrake	Hazard awareness	Air conditioning
Use of gears	Separation distances	Monitor fuel efficiency
Speed choice	Use of engine braking	Vehicle servicing
	Use of cruise control	Reducing wear on vehicle
	Stopping engine when appropriate	Reducing CO_2
	Warm engine for reversing manoeuvres	

Preparation Notes:

Review previous learning, including theory elements.

Driving styles, consideration for other road users and coping with incidents of aggressive behaviour.

Essentials:

Adapt a smooth driving style with good forward planning and anticipation.

Location:

All roads.

Goals for Driver Education (GDE) matrix

Level 1, 2, 3 & 4

National standard for driving cars and light vans:

Role 2: Guide and control the vehicle

Role 3: Use the road in accordance with the Highway Code

Role 4: Drive safely and responsibly in the traffic system

Anything else?

You decide ...

I really struggle with this	I need to be better at this	I am okay at this	I am pretty good at this	This is a real strength of mine
1	2	3	4	5

Lesson 17: Independent Driving

Introducing Key Learning Areas

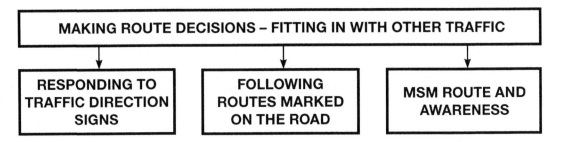

MAKING ROUTE DECISIONS – FITTING IN WITH OTHER TRAFFIC		
RESPONDING TO TRAFFIC DIRECTION SIGNS	FOLLOWING ROUTES MARKED ON THE ROAD	MSM ROUTE AND AWARENESS

Preparation Notes:
Learner judged to be ready to drive a route without guidance or any training input

Essentials:
Apply "Mirrors – Signal – Manoeuvre" routine fully independently.

Location:
All roads.

Goals for Driver Education (GDE) matrix
Level 2, 3 & 4

National standard for driving cars and light vans:
Role 2: Guide and control the vehicle

Role 3: Use the road in accordance with the Highway Code

Role 4: Drive safely and responsibly in the traffic system

Anything else?
You decide …

I really struggle with this	I need to be better at this	I am okay at this	I am pretty good at this	This is a real strength of mine
1	2	3	4	5

Lesson 18: Traffic Signs, Signals and Road Markings

Introducing Key Learning Areas

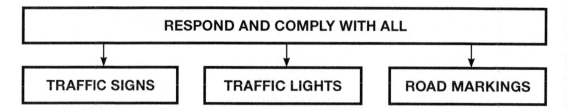

Preparation Notes:

Review of "Know Your Traffic Signs" booklet …

1. Ability to recognise traffic signs and road markings

2. Compliance with mandatory direction and other signs

Driving styles, consideration for other road users and coping with incidents of aggressive behaviour.

Essentials:

Apply previous theory learning eg. showing understanding of traffic sign and signal types

Apply "Mirrors – Signal – Manoeuvre" routine to individual circumstances.

Location:

All roads, including one-way traffic systems

Goals for Driver Education (GDE) matrix

Level 2, 3 & 4

National standard for driving cars and light vans:

Role 2: Guide and control the vehicle

Role 3: Use the road in accordance with the Highway Code

Role 4: Drive safely and responsibly in the traffic system

Anything else?

You decide ...

I really struggle with this	I need to be better at this	I am okay at this	I am pretty good at this	This is a real strength of mine
1	2	3	4	5

Lesson 19: Satellite Navigation

Introducing Key Learning Areas

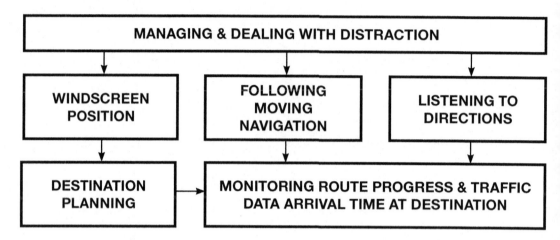

Preparation Notes:

- Reason for this lesson topic

- Programming the sat nav

- Link with independent driving

- Outcome of taking the wrong route

Consider risk of trusting satellite navigation systems too much – Possibility that we think less for ourselves. We are driving, not the SatNav. We cannot blame this device if we have a collision or commit an offence.

Essentials:

Apply "Mirrors – Signal – Manoeuvre" routine fully independently.

Location:

All roads.

Goals for Driver Education (GDE) matrix

Level 1, 2, 3 & 4

National standard for driving cars and light vans:

Role 2: Guide and control the vehicle

Role 3: Use the road in accordance with the Highway Code

Role 4: Drive safely and responsibly in the traffic system

Anything else?

You decide …

I really struggle with this	I need to be better at this	I am okay at this	I am pretty good at this	This is a real strength of mine
1	2	3	4	5

Lesson 20: Reversing

Introducing Key Learning Areas

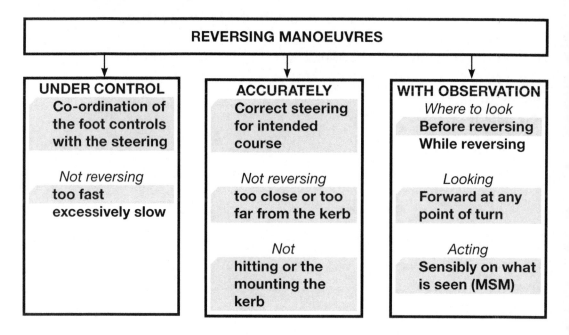

REVERSING MANOEUVRES

UNDER CONTROL	ACCURATELY	WITH OBSERVATION
Co-ordination of the foot controls with the steering	Correct steering for intended course	*Where to look* Before reversing While reversing
Not reversing too fast excessively slow	*Not reversing* too close or too far from the kerb	*Looking* Forward at any point of turn
	Not hitting or the mounting the kerb	*Acting* Sensibly on what is seen (MSM)

Preparation Notes:

Revisiting the skills associated with moving and stopping the car, but this time including driving backwards.

Reversing Manoeuvres:

1. Reversing in a straight line

2. Reversing around a left or right corner

3. Reverse parking

4. Bay parking

5. Pull up on the right, reverse and re-join the traffic

Essentials:
- Use diagram
- "Explain – Demonstrate – Practice" (EDP) Method
- "Preparation – Observation – Manouevre" (POM) Routine

Location:
Quiet flat road

Goals for Driver Education (GDE) matrix
Level 1

National standard for driving cars and light vans:
Role 1 Preparing the vehicle for a journey

Role 2: Guide and control the vehicle:

Anything else?
You decide …

I really struggle with this	I need to be better at this	I am okay at this	I am pretty good at this	This is a real strength of mine
1	2	3	4	5

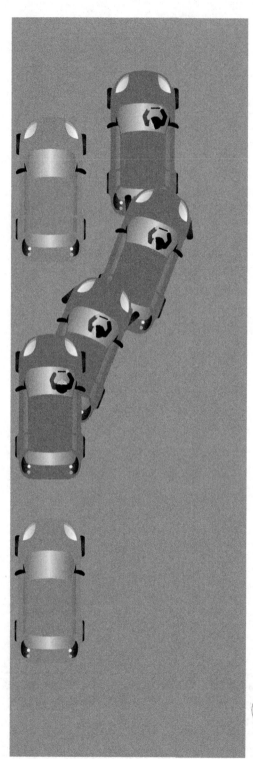

Lesson 21: Parking

Introducing Key Learning Areas

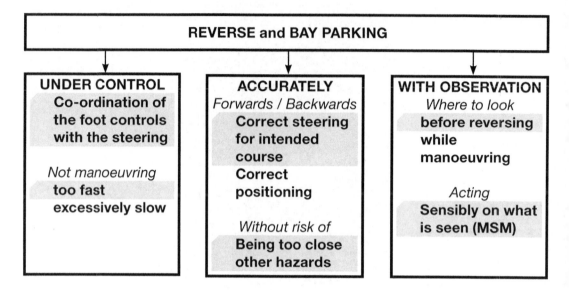

REVERSE and BAY PARKING		
UNDER CONTROL **Co-ordination of the foot controls with the steering** *Not manoeuvring* **too fast** **excessively slow**	**ACCURATELY** *Forwards / Backwards* **Correct steering for intended course** **Correct positioning** *Without risk of* **Being too close other hazards**	**WITH OBSERVATION** *Where to look* **before reversing while manoeuvring** *Acting* **Sensibly on what is seen (MSM)**

Preparation Notes:

Adapting manoeuvring skills for this everyday exercise.

Essentials:

- Use diagram
- "Explain – Demonstrate – Practice" (EDP) Method
- "Preparation – Observation – Manoeuvre" (POM) Routine

Location:

Quiet flat road

Goals for Driver Education (GDE) matrix

Level 1

National standard for driving cars and light vans:

Role 1 Preparing the vehicle for a journey

Role 2: Guide and control the vehicle:

Anything else?

You decide ...

I really struggle with this	I need to be better at this	I am okay at this	I am pretty good at this	This is a real strength of mine
1	2	3	4	5

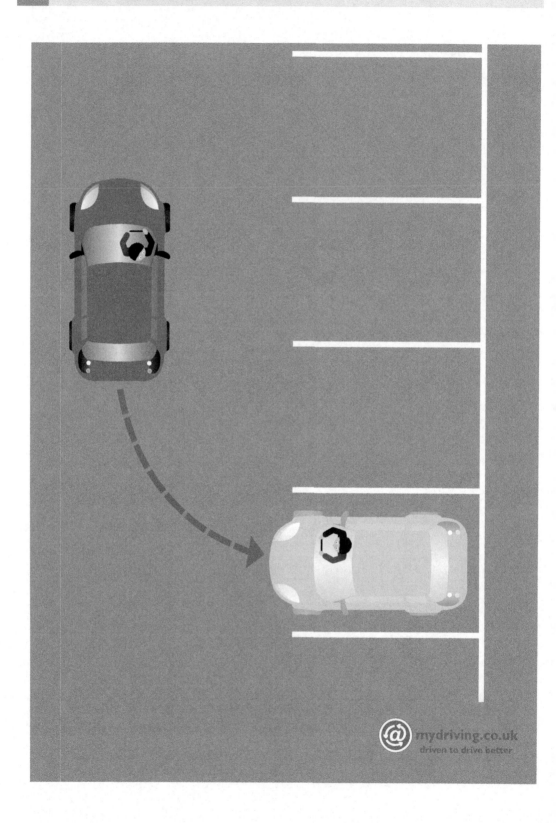

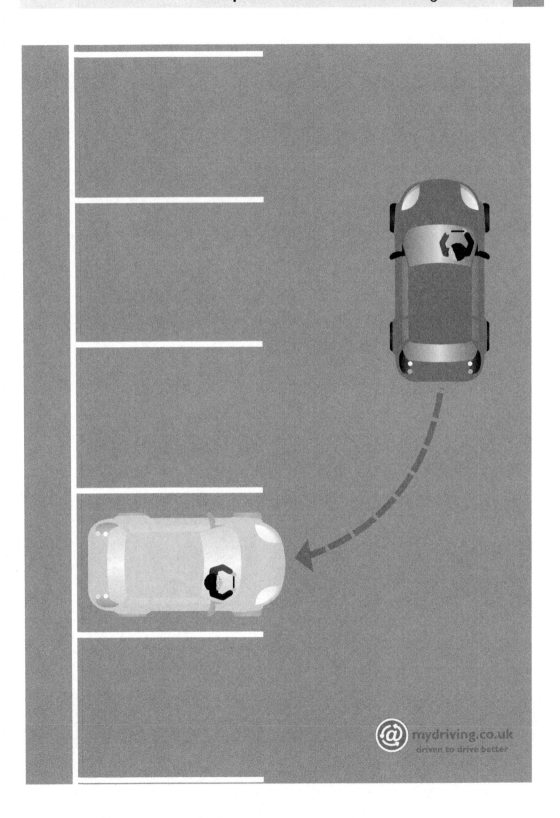

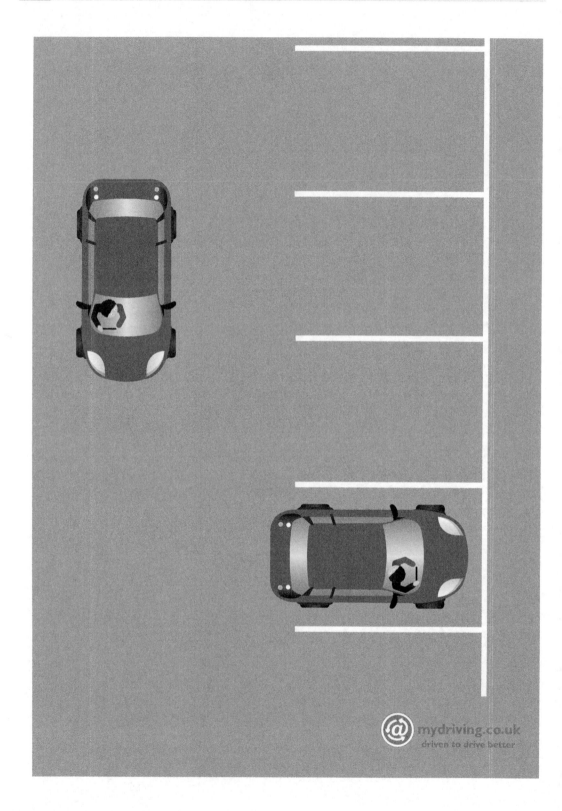

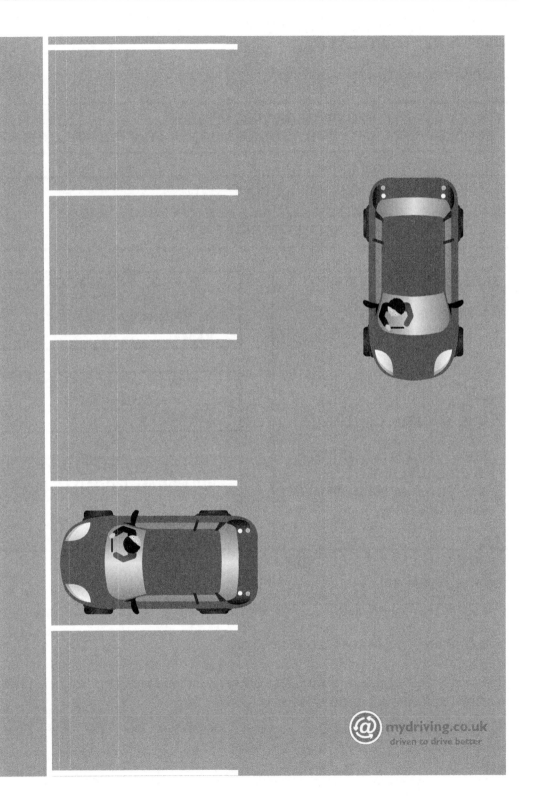

Lesson 22: Town Driving

Consolidation of Key Learning Areas

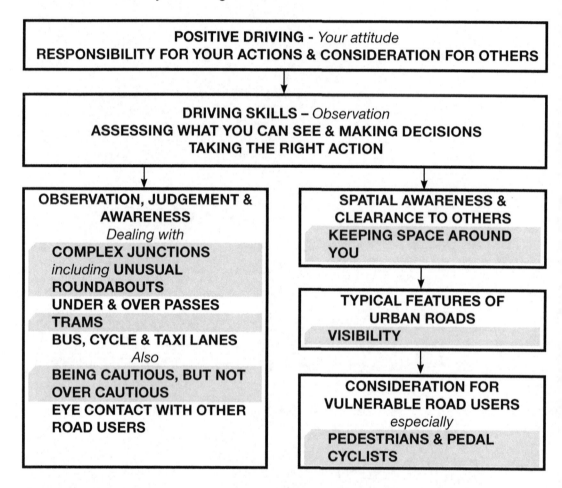

POSITIVE DRIVING - *Your attitude*
RESPONSIBILITY FOR YOUR ACTIONS & CONSIDERATION FOR OTHERS

DRIVING SKILLS – *Observation*
**ASSESSING WHAT YOU CAN SEE & MAKING DECISIONS
TAKING THE RIGHT ACTION**

OBSERVATION, JUDGEMENT & AWARENESS
Dealing with
COMPLEX JUNCTIONS
including **UNUSUAL ROUNDABOUTS
UNDER & OVER PASSES
TRAMS
BUS, CYCLE & TAXI LANES**
Also
**BEING CAUTIOUS, BUT NOT OVER CAUTIOUS
EYE CONTACT WITH OTHER ROAD USERS**

**SPATIAL AWARENESS & CLEARANCE TO OTHERS
KEEPING SPACE AROUND YOU**

**TYPICAL FEATURES OF URBAN ROADS
VISIBILITY**

CONSIDERATION FOR VULNERABLE ROAD USERS
especially
PEDESTRIANS & PEDAL CYCLISTS

Preparation Notes:

Judgment approaching road hazards

Good forward planning and anticipation.

Driving styles, consideration for other road users and coping with incidents of aggressive behaviour.

Essentials:

- Apply "Mirrors – Signal – Manoeuvre" routine to individual circumstances.

- Hierarchy of road users

Location:

All roads.

Goals for Driver Education (GDE) matrix

Level 2, 3 & 4

National standard for driving cars and light vans:

Roles 2, 3, 4 & 5

Anything else?

You decide ...

I really struggle with this	I need to be better at this	I am okay at this	I am pretty good at this	This is a real strength of mine
1	2	3	4	5

Lesson 23: All Weather Driving

Consolidation of Key Learning Areas

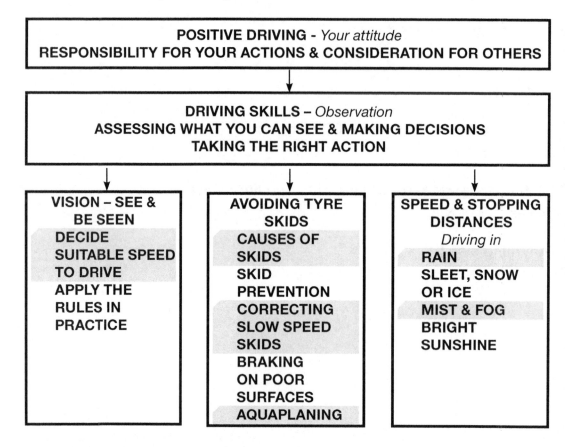

POSITIVE DRIVING - *Your attitude*
RESPONSIBILITY FOR YOUR ACTIONS & CONSIDERATION FOR OTHERS

DRIVING SKILLS – *Observation*
ASSESSING WHAT YOU CAN SEE & MAKING DECISIONS
TAKING THE RIGHT ACTION

| VISION – SEE & BE SEEN DECIDE SUITABLE SPEED TO DRIVE APPLY THE RULES IN PRACTICE | AVOIDING TYRE SKIDS CAUSES OF SKIDS SKID PREVENTION CORRECTING SLOW SPEED SKIDS BRAKING ON POOR SURFACES AQUAPLANING | SPEED & STOPPING DISTANCES *Driving in* RAIN SLEET, SNOW OR ICE MIST & FOG BRIGHT SUNSHINE |

Preparation Notes:

Judgment, good forward planning and anticipation.

Driving styles, consideration for other road users and coping with incidents of aggressive behaviour.

Essentials:

Apply "Mirrors – Signal – Manoeuvre" routine to individual circumstances.

Location:

All roads.

Goals for Driver Education (GDE) matrix

Level 2, 3 & 4

National standard for driving cars and light vans:

Roles 1, 2, 3, 4 & 5

Anything else?

You decide ...

I really struggle with this	I need to be better at this	I am okay at this	I am pretty good at this	This is a real strength of mine
1	2	3	4	5

Lesson 24: Out of Town Driving and Rural Roads

Consolidation of Key Learning Areas

POSITIVE DRIVING - *Your attitude*
RESPONSIBILITY FOR YOUR ACTIONS & CONSIDERATION FOR OTHERS

↓

DRIVING SKILLS – *Observation*
ASSESSING WHAT YOU CAN SEE & MAKING DECISIONS
TAKING THE RIGHT ACTION

↓ ↓ ↓

RURAL HAZARDS	OVERTAKING &	OBSERVATION
COUNTRY	PROGRESS	SKILLS
LANES	FOLLOWING	*Anticipation of*
BENDS	DISTANCES	PEDESTRIANS
UNEVEN ROADS	SAFE	WALKING IN THE
DEAD GROUND	OVERTAKING	ROAD
ROADS WITHOUT	PROCEDURE	HORSE RIDERS
PAVEMENTS	PASSING	SLOW VEHICLES
FARM	PLACES	LIKESTOCK &
ENTRANCES &	MAKING SAFE	WILD ANIMALS
BUILDINGS	PROGRESS	IN THE ROAD
MUD OR DEBRIS		
ON THE ROAD		

Preparation Notes:

Judgment approaching road hazards

Good forward planning and anticipation.

Driving styles, consideration for other road users and coping with incidents of aggressive behaviour.

Essentials:

- Apply "Mirrors – Signal – Manoeuvre" routine to individual circumstances.

- Hierarchy of road users

Location:

All roads.

Goals for Driver Education (GDE) matrix

Level 2, 3 & 4

National standard for driving cars and light vans:

Roles 2, 3, 4 & 5

Anything else?

You decide ...

I really struggle with this	I need to be better at this	I am okay at this	I am pretty good at this	This is a real strength of mine
1	2	3	4	5

Lesson 25: Night Driving

Consolidation of Key Learning Areas

POSITIVE DRIVING - *Your attitude*
RESPONSIBILITY FOR YOUR ACTIONS & CONSIDERATION FOR OTHERS

↓

DRIVING SKILLS – *Observation*
ASSESSING WHAT YOU CAN SEE & MAKING DECISIONS **TAKING THE RIGHT ACTION**

↓ ↓ ↓

VEHICLE LIGHTING & USE	SPEED & STOPPING DISTANCES	VISIBILITY – SEEING & REACTING SAFELY
Checking that all **LIGHTS ARE CLEAN** *Use of headlights when driving* **AT DUSK** **IN THE DARK** **AT DAWN** *Use of lights when* **PARKING AT NIGHT** *How to avoid* **DAZZLING OTHER DRIVERS**	*Judging* **OWN SPEED & DISTANCES AT NIGHT** **OTHER VEHICLES' SPEED & DISTANCES AT NIGHT**	*Awareness & Anticipation of* **PEDESTRIANS PEDAL CYCLISTS & OTHER ROAD USERS** **OTHER DRIVERS WHO DAZZLE YOU**

Preparation Notes:

Judgment approaching road hazards

Good forward planning and anticipation.

Driving styles, consideration for other road users and coping with incidents of aggressive behaviour.

Essentials:
Apply "Mirrors – Signal – Manoeuvre" routine to individual circumstances.

Location:
All roads.

Goals for Driver Education (GDE) matrix
Level 2, 3 & 4

National standard for driving cars and light vans:
Roles 2, 3, 4 & 5

Anything else?
You decide …

I really struggle with this	I need to be better at this	I am okay at this	I am pretty good at this	This is a real strength of mine
1	2	3	4	5

Lesson 26: Dual Carriageways

Consolidation of Key Learning Areas

POSITIVE DRIVING - *Your attitude*
RESPONSIBILITY FOR YOUR ACTIONS & CONSIDERATION FOR OTHERS

↓

DRIVING SKILLS – *Observation*
ASSESSING WHAT YOU CAN SEE & MAKING DECISIONS
TAKING THE RIGHT ACTION

JOINING & LEAVING
TRAFFIC SIGNS:
PRIMARY &
NON-PRIMARY
ROUTES
JOINING:
EFFECTIVE
OBSERVATION
LEAVING:
RETURN TO
TWO-WAY ROADS
& POSSIBLE
CHANGE OF
SPEED LIMIT
USE OF SLIP
ROADS

FORWARD PLANNING & OBSERVATION
EFFECTIVE OBSERVATION INCLUDING
USE OF MIRRORS & BLINDSPOTS
SCANNING NEAR, MIDDLE & FAR
DISTANCE
ACTING ON TRAFFIC SIGNS, SIGNALS
& ROAD MARKINGS
APPROPRIATE USE OF SPEED IN
DIFFERENT CIRCUMSTANCES
FOLLOWING DISTANCES INCLUDING
THE TWO SECOND RULE
COURTESY TO OTHER ROAD USERS
USE OF LIGHTS, INCLUDING
HEADLIGHTS & HAZARD LIGHTS

OVERTAKING
KEEPING DISTANCE / SPACE & LANE
DISCIPLINE

Preparation Notes:

Judgment, good forward planning and anticipation.

Driving styles, consideration for other road users and coping with incidents of aggressive behaviour.

Essentials:

Apply "Mirrors – Signal – Manoeuvre" routine to individual circumstances.

Location:

All roads.

Goals for Driver Education (GDE) matrix

Level 2, 3 & 4

National standard for driving cars and light vans:

Roles 2, 3, 4 & 5

Anything else?

You decide …

I really struggle with this	I need to be better at this	I am okay at this	I am pretty good at this	This is a real strength of mine
1	2	3	4	5

Lesson 27: Motorways

Consolidation of Key Learning Areas

POSITIVE DRIVING - *Your attitude*
RESPONSIBILITY FOR YOUR ACTIONS & CONSIDERATION FOR OTHERS

DRIVING SKILLS – *Observation*
ASSESSING WHAT YOU CAN SEE & MAKING DECISIONS
TAKING THE RIGHT ACTION

JOINING & LEAVING
TRAFFIC SIGNS:
PRIMARY &
NON-PRIMARY
ROUTES
JOINING:
EFFECTIVE
OBSERVATION
LEAVING
PROCEDURE:
RETURN
PRIMARY /
NON-PRIMARY
ROUTES / DUAL
CARRIAGEWAY
OR TWO-WAY
ROADS &
POSSIBLE
CHANGE OF
SPEED LIMIT
USE OF SLIP
ROADS

FORWARD PLANNING
& OBSERVATION
EFFECTIVE
OBSERVATION
INCLUDING USE
OF MIRRORS &
BLINDSPOTS
SCANNING NEAR,
MIDDLE & FAR
DISTANCE
ACTING ON
TRAFFIC SIGNS,
SIGNALS & ROAD
MARKINGS
APPROPRIATE
USE OF SPEED
IN DIFFERENT
CIRCUMSTANCES
FOLLOWING
DISTANCES
INCLUDING THE 2
SECOND RULE
COURTESY TO
OTHER TRAFFIC
USE OF LIGHTS,
INCLUDING
HEADLIGHTS &
HAZARD LIGHTS

OVERTAKING
KEEPING
DISTANCE /
SPACE
LANE
DISCIPLINE

**BREAKDOWN &
SAFETY PROCEDURE**
HIGHWAY CODE
ADVICE
SMART
MOTORWAYS

Preparation Notes:
Judgment, good forward planning and anticipation.

Driving styles, consideration for other road users and coping with incidents of aggressive behaviour.

Essentials:
Apply "Mirrors – Signal – Manoeuvre" routine to individual circumstances.

Location:
All roads.

Goals for Driver Education (GDE) matrix
Level 2, 3 & 4

National standard for driving cars and light vans:
Roles 2, 3, 4 & 5

Anything else?
You decide …

I really struggle with this	I need to be better at this	I am okay at this	I am pretty good at this	This is a real strength of mine
1	2	3	4	5

Lesson 28: Advanced Driving

Key Learning Areas

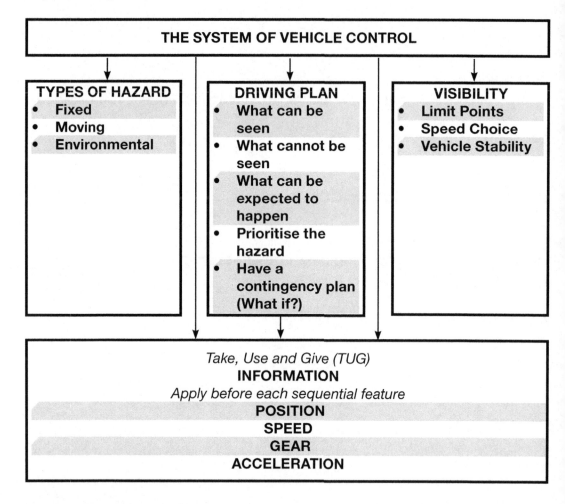

THE SYSTEM OF VEHICLE CONTROL		
TYPES OF HAZARD • Fixed • Moving • Environmental	**DRIVING PLAN** • What can be seen • What cannot be seen • What can be expected to happen • Prioritise the hazard • Have a contingency plan (What if?)	**VISIBILITY** • Limit Points • Speed Choice • Vehicle Stability

Take, Use and Give (TUG)
INFORMATION
Apply before each sequential feature
POSITION
SPEED
GEAR
ACCELERATION

Preparation Notes:

"System" – Use Roadcraft.

Judgment, good forward planning and anticipation.

Driving styles, consideration for other road users and coping with incidents of aggressive behaviour.

Essentials:

Apply "Mirrors – Signal – Manoeuvre" routine to individual circumstances.

Location:

All roads.

Goals for Driver Education (GDE) matrix

Level 2, 3 & 4

National standard for driving cars and light vans:

Roles 2, 3, 4 & 5

Anything else?

You decide ...

I really struggle with this	I need to be better at this	I am okay at this	I am pretty good at this	This is a real strength of mine
1	2	3	4	5

Lesson 29: Corporate Driving

Key Learning Areas

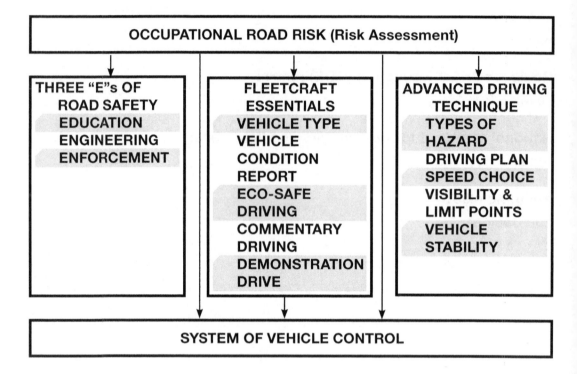

OCCUPATIONAL ROAD RISK (Risk Assessment)

THREE "E"s OF ROAD SAFETY	FLEETCRAFT ESSENTIALS	ADVANCED DRIVING TECHNIQUE
EDUCATION	VEHICLE TYPE	TYPES OF
ENGINEERING	VEHICLE	HAZARD
ENFORCEMENT	CONDITION	DRIVING PLAN
	REPORT	SPEED CHOICE
	ECO-SAFE	VISIBILITY &
	DRIVING	LIMIT POINTS
	COMMENTARY	VEHICLE
	DRIVING	STABILITY
	DEMONSTRATION	
	DRIVE	

SYSTEM OF VEHICLE CONTROL

Preparation Notes:

"System" – Use Roadcraft.

Judgment, good forward planning and anticipation.

Driving styles, consideration for other road users and coping with incidents of aggressive behaviour.

Essentials:

Apply "Mirrors – Signal – Manoeuvre" routine to individual circumstances.

Location:

All roads.

Goals for Driver Education (GDE) matrix

Level 2, 3 & 4

National standard for driving cars and light vans:

Roles 2, 3, 4 & 5

Anything else?

You decide ...

I really struggle with this	I need to be better at this	I am okay at this	I am pretty good at this	This is a real strength of mine
1	2	3	4	5

Lesson 30: Towing a trailer / Lorry & Bus driving

Key Learning Areas

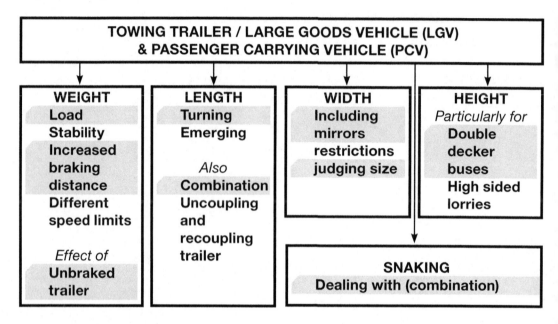

TOWING TRAILER / LARGE GOODS VEHICLE (LGV) & PASSENGER CARRYING VEHICLE (PCV)

WEIGHT
Load
Stability
Increased braking distance
Different speed limits

Effect of
Unbraked trailer

LENGTH
Turning
Emerging

Also
Combination
Uncoupling and recoupling trailer

WIDTH
Including mirrors restrictions
judging size

HEIGHT
Particularly for
Double decker buses
High sided lorries

SNAKING
Dealing with (combination)

PRE-SET MANOEUVRE

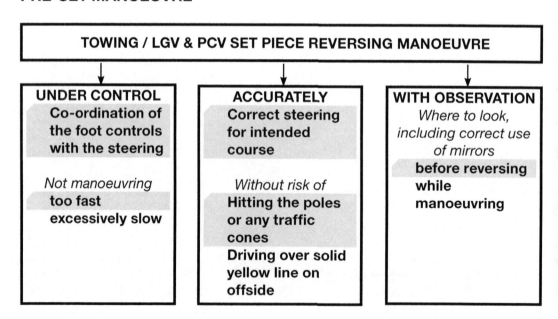

TOWING / LGV & PCV SET PIECE REVERSING MANOEUVRE

UNDER CONTROL
Co-ordination of the foot controls with the steering

Not manoeuvring
too fast
excessively slow

ACCURATELY
Correct steering for intended course

Without risk of
Hitting the poles or any traffic cones
Driving over solid yellow line on offside

WITH OBSERVATION
Where to look, including correct use of mirrors
before reversing while manoeuvring

Preparation Notes:

Adapt and tailor previous car Lesson Plans to learner's specific needs.

Driving styles, consideration for other road users and coping with incidents of aggressive behaviour.

Essentials:

- Apply "Mirrors – Signal – Manoeuvre" routine to individual circumstances.

- Hierarchy of road users

Location:

All roads.

Goals for Driver Education (GDE) matrix

Level 2, 3 & 4

National standard for driving lorries (Category C) / buses and coaches (Category D)

Roles 1, 2, 3, 4 & 5

Anything else?

You decide ...

I really struggle with this	I need to be better at this	I am okay at this	I am pretty good at this	This is a real strength of mine
1	2	3	4	5

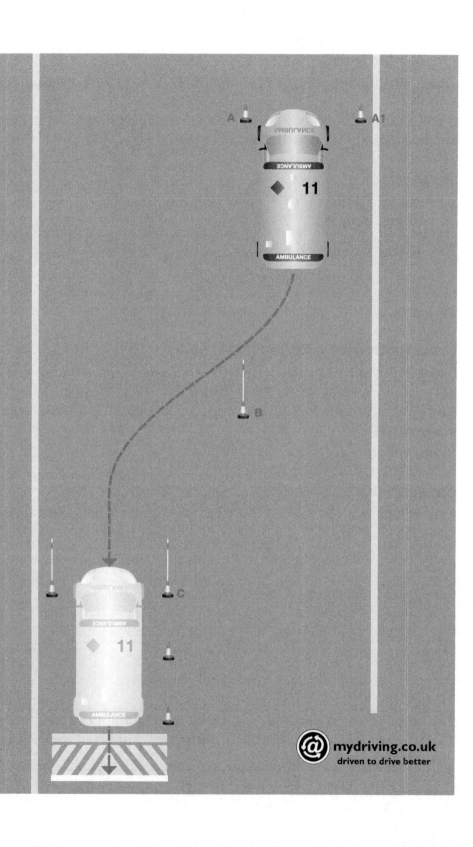

CHAPTER 10

HOW TO GET MORE OUT OF YOUR ADI QUALIFICATION

**Self Development & Business
Opportunities**

Continuing Professional Development (CPD)

You will have worked extremely hard to become an Approved Driving Instructor. To keep your knowledge up to date, as well as your personal driving and teaching skills, it is worth investing some time in your own Continuing Professional Development.

The DVSA recommend that driver trainers commit themselves to at least seven hours of continuing professional development each year. This is the same amount of time that is mandatory for bus and lorry driver CPC (Continuing Professional Competence).

There are different forms of CPD, ranging from self-update to participating in online events, or actual course attendance. However, it is estimated that only 5-10% of instructors take part in any formal CPD. This is disappointing and leaves ADIs in a vulnerable position professionally, potentially becoming outdated in their procedures and practices. With this in mind, it is a good idea to prioritise and decide what you need to do better. Here are some ideas:

BUSINESS CPD

Once qualified, the most important professional development must be managing your own business successfully. Teaching someone to drive has great rewards, especially when someone that you have taught from the beginning passes first time, without any driving faults being recorded. If you do not have another customer to replace each test success, then your talents are not only being wasted, but your business will not succeed.

A successful business must have a continuous flow of new customers. To ensure this, you will need to devise and properly implement a business plan. This will include ways to attract new customers to your school, as well as how to keep them.

SAFEGUARDING CPD

Anyone that comes into contact or works with children, young people or vulnerable adults requires a knowledge of safeguarding. This includes awareness of a person's right to live in safety, free from abuse, harm or neglect.

TECHNICAL CPD

Teaching learners regularly can have a negative impact on your own driving, so it is worthwhile considering taking one or more of the advanced driving tests with such organisations as the Institute of Advanced Motorists (IAM), Royal Society for the Prevention of Accidents (RoSPA), or the Driving Instructors' Association (DIA). Re-tests are also a good idea, which RoSPA include automatically for their members. The DVSA also run the "Cardington Special Driving Test" for ADIs. This is assessed at the same high level used when training new driving examiners.

The DIA offer a five-part examination known as the "Diploma in Driving Instruction". It is a test of knowledge covering:

1. Legal obligations and regulations.

2. Management practices and procedures.

3. Vehicle maintenance and mechanical principles.

4. Driving theory, skills, and procedures.

5. Instructing practices and procedures.

A certificate is issued for each module and the diploma is awarded when all five modules have been completed. Broadly speaking, other forms of technical CPD are divided into two main types:

1. **Course or webinar attendance**

    National ADI organisations such as the Motor Schools Association (MSA), the Driving Instructors Association (DIA), and the ADI Joint Council (ADINJC) run nationwide bespoke CPD courses that will be of genuine interest to most ADIs. Other courses are also available such as BTECs. These include an award in "Driving Science" and "Coaching for Driver Education".

2. **Event attendance**

   Road safety organisations such as the Royal Society for the Prevention of Accidents (RoSPA) and the Association for Road Risk Management (ARRM)—formerly the Association of Industrial Road Safety Officers (AIRSO)—organise regular events that can be of interest to ADIs. These are a good way of broadening a driver trainer's perspective beyond the training of novice drivers.

Whether you attend a course, or an event such as a conference or a seminar, the organisations hosting these will usually provide an attendance certificate that contributes towards your voluntary CPD. In line with the mandatory "Driver Certificate of Professional Competence" (DCPC) for bus and lorry drivers, ADIs are officially being encouraged to complete and record at least seven hours of CPD annually. You may wish to have your CPD certificates available when you take your "Standards Check".

QUALIFIED DRIVER TRAINING

The core business for most ADIs is teaching learner drivers. But, one way to progress your career is to vary and diversify your work into **other** areas of driver training.

On 6th February 1995, the DVSA introduced a scheme for newly qualified drivers to take further training to help reduce the risk of costly collisions. "Pass Plus" is a voluntary scheme that is an excellent way for new instructors to start getting experience training qualified drivers, as well as generating extra business income.

With the driving test out of the way, you can adapt more of a coaching approach to the development sessions. Using the DVSA's "Pass Plus" syllabus you can deal with the possibility of negative emotions such as anxiety, stress, fear, guilt, embarrassment, intimidation, and frustration. Teaching new drivers to balance making progress on the road with being cautious and ignoring passenger-peer taunts is important to building confidence, self-esteem, and self-belief, while keeping the car under control and totally safe.

The "Pass Plus" scheme for car drivers:

- "Pass Plus" is designed to help new drivers gain quality practical driving experience.

- Statistics show that new drivers are far more likely to have a collision in the first two years after passing their test.

- Traffic collisions are the single greatest killer of 15-24 year-olds. This age range of drivers is greatly over-represented in single-car and loss of control crashes, and collisions where the driver is turning across oncoming traffic.

- Every week, around 300 driving licences are revoked, where new drivers have gained six penalty points within two years of passing their driving tests. This totals more than 15,000 every year.

- The official course can only be offered by ADIs who have registered with the DVSA for the scheme. The current fee for this is £37. Refill packs are charged at £29.

- The course is designed to take at least 6 one-hour practical sessions. However, local conditions and time of year may mean that some modules need to be given as a theory session. A theory session could be given in circumstances where there is no motorway nearby. As a rule, at least five and a half out of six hours should be spent in the car.

- Local authorities may offer help with the "Pass Plus" course fees.

- The instructor sets the course fees.

"Pass Plus" consists of six separate modules:

1. Town Driving (Including "Pass Plus" Induction)

2. All Weather Driving

3. Out of Town Driving and Rural Roads

4. Night Driving

5. Dual Carriageway

6. Motorway Driving

When this scheme was first introduced, over 25 years ago, over 12% of new drivers took up the course. This has now fallen considerably, as the insurance reductions offered to new drivers for completing the course are disappointing. However, you should ideally encourage your pupils to take some advanced driver training after their test success, not only for their own benefits and road safety, but also to improve your income stream.

REFRESHER COURSES

Refresher driving lessons or courses are usually short, where the training is designed to fulfil a particular individual need. The course will normally employ key skills such as better awareness, anticipation, and planning. Such skills enable a driver to read the road better, and as a result will reduce wear and tear on a vehicle and reduce fuel consumption. Each course should be structured to suit specific learning requirements such as:

1. **Nervous drivers**. For example, someone who has recently passed the test but still feels too nervous to drive alone. Your customer could be someone who has been involved in a traffic collision and is nervous about the prospect of driving again. Refresher courses for nervous drivers will need to begin in a quiet location and gradually build up to busier and more complex traffic conditions, but only at a rate that the driver feels comfortable with. The aim will be to boost the driver's confidence, particularly in the traffic conditions they are likely to experience.

2. **Senior drivers**. More than seven million drivers are over 65, of which four and a half million are aged 70 or over. With the gradually increasing number of elderly drivers on the road, some may feel they will benefit from refresher training. As a driver must legally renew their licence at the age of 70, plus every three years after this, it is the driver themselves who determines whether they are fit to drive. Refresher driving lessons for the elderly offer the driver increased confidence in their abilities by eliminating bad habits and increasing hazard awareness. Such courses are not intended to prevent or discourage elderly drivers from staying behind the wheel.

3. **Non-UK residents**. An overseas licence holder may legitimately drive in the UK for up to twelve months on their full licence. One of the dilemmas visitors to Britain face is that if they intend on driving, they will not be familiar with driving on the left. The majority of countries drive on the right, so driving on the other side of the road is likely to be daunting without a little professional tuition. The high frequency in which roundabouts are used in the UK can also pose an issue to many who may only come across them rarely.

4. **New UK residents**. The UK has a driving licence exchange agreement with 50 other countries. 32 of the approved countries drive on the right. Since 1997, over a million foreign drivers have exchanged their own licences for a UK one. This has increased substantially, suggesting that this is growing market. Training should build on their previous driving experience and be tailored to the "Highway Code".

5. **Drivers needing to take an Extended Driving Test**. Where a qualified driver is disqualified for certain serious driving offences, a court can order that once the disqualification period has ended, the individual must return to provisional driving licence status. To gain or regain a full licence, the driver must go through the entire driving test process as a learner driver does. This also includes taking the theory test.

The extended driving test is more challenging than the ordinary learner driver's test. It is not necessarily harder, but it lasts twice as long and involves doing more; therefore there is a higher possibility of something going wrong. Customers need to be prepared to complete all the manoeuvres, including reversing and emergency stops. There are around 5,000 extended tests carried out every year, and the pass rate is over 15% higher than the learner car test.

Training will need to begin with an assessment and should then progress as with any other refresher course. Candidates will expect to be given an analysis of their ability, along with an estimate of how many further lessons/sessions are required.

DISABLED DRIVERS

Within the terms of the Disability and Equality Act 2010, ADIs may be legally obliged to provide training to someone with impairment. Teaching disabled people to drive can be exceptionally rewarding. Gaining a full driving licence often helps a disabled driver to gain more freedom and independence, and therefore you can be assured that they will work very hard to accomplish this goal. There are some excellent courses available for ADIs who wish to specialise in this area. You can expect to cover such areas as:

- The various types of disabilities & physical conditions.
- Teaching techniques for people with physical disabilities, learning difficulties, and hearing impairment.
- Knowledge on medical conditions.
- The effects of cognitive impairments.
- Older drivers.
- Driving various adapted vehicles.
- Vehicle conversion specialists.
- Wheelchair seating, loading, management & stowage.
- Visual problems and testing vision.
- Aspects of modifications, licences, insurance & driving tests.

A list of mobility centres, including the Queen Elizabeth Foundation (QEF), is given in *Driving: The Essential Skills*.

TOWING TRAILERS

Following a change to legislation in September 2021, car licence holders can now tow trailers. Those who are new to towing are strongly encouraged to take training before going out on the road with a trailer – though this is not mandatory. For the driver trainer, the National Standard for Driving

Cars & Light Vans are a "must read". These set out the full range of skills and knowledge needed for towing a trailer.

ADVANCED AND CORPORATE DRIVER TRAINING

With around 32 million full licence holders in the UK, opportunities do exist in the qualified driver training sector. The legal obligations for employers to ensure that employees driving for work have their driving checked, have created opportunities for enterprising ADIs. You can canvas for this work, beginning with your local Chamber of Commerce; businesses; schools; colleges; health authorities, along with voluntary and charity groups. By becoming DVSA fleet registered, you will gain a professional advantage.

Work also exists on specialist training courses for drivers of all terrain 4x4 vehicles; and high performance cars including racetrack experience and antihijacking techniques. Assessment and training opportunities may exist within NHS Patient Transport Services (PTS) or private ambulance services.

There are several national companies, such as the AA who own the BSM brand, the advanced motoring organisations, including the Institute of Advanced Motorists (IAM) and the Royal Society for the Prevention of Accidents (RoSPA), who offer corporate driver training and development. Competition amongst experienced ADIs to get this work can be quite tough, and you may be expected to pay for an additional training course so that you meet corporate "brand requirements". You will most certainly need to produce a professional CV that reflects all your talents, skills, abilities, and relevant experience.

DRIVER INTERVENTION SCHEMES

Driver education courses are run with the support of the police as an alternative to the fixed penalty points system or court prosecution. The offender pays a course fee.

There are a range of National Driver Offender Retraining Scheme (NDORS) courses for certain road traffic offences, including:

1. **National Speed Awareness Course.** This where the offence is excess speed, and is within a given percentage of the posted limit. This course has a four-hour duration.

2. **Safe and Considerate Driving (SCD).** A whole-day course where the offence relates to careless driving (driving without due care and attention).

3. **What's Driving Us?** A half-day course, as an alternative to both fixed penalty and endorsable offences. Examples include tailgating, traffic light offences, crossing a solid white line, stopping, overtaking, or failing to give precedence in zebra/puffin/pelican areas, stopping at school gates, and contravening a no-entry sign.

4. **National Motorway Awareness Course.** Here the driver has committed an offence on a motorway, such as driving on the hard shoulder or failing to comply with the red X. This course has a duration of three hours and 45 minutes.

5. **Drink Drive Rehabilitation Scheme**. This post-court course reduces the length of ban by up to 25%. This course has a duration of 16 hours, spread out over three to four days.

Courses are predominantly classroom based or can be online. They are often run by Local Authority Road Safety Departments, or by private companies, who are contracted or appointed as service providers for their respective Police Authorities. Competition amongst experienced ADIs to get this work can be quite tough, and you can be expected to have additional teaching qualifications relevant to managing the classroom environment.

Professional Development Plan (PDP). In a bid to achieve mastery and increase work opportunities, it is worth considering formal adult teaching qualifications such as:

• **Level 3 Award in Education and Training.** This was previously "Preparing to Teach in the Lifelong Learning Sector" (PTLLS).

- **Level 4 Certificate in Education and Training.** This was previously "Certificate in Teaching in the Lifelong Learning Sector" (CTLLS).

- **Level 5 Diploma in Education and Training.** This was previously "Diploma in Teaching in the Lifelong Learning Sector" (DTLLS).

These awards are managed within the National Qualifications Framework (NQF). Level 3 is seen as equivalent to an A-Level, while Level 4 is a next step achievement into Higher Education.

BECOMING FLEET QUALIFIED

Since April 2002, as part of the Government's "Road Safety Strategy", the DVSA have run a separate voluntary "fleet" register of ADIs who specialise in the training and development of company car drivers. The work is described in different ways, such as "occupational road risk", "corporate driver improvement" or "collision risk management".

The business potential for fleet ADIs is as big as there are companies with drivers working for them. The key to business success is being able to access this market. In terms of your competition, the growth in number of fleet-registered instructors has been very gradual, but there are still only round 3,000 ADIs.

There are two routes to becoming a fleet trainer. To prepare and qualify for this kind of work, most instructors take an accredited fleet course with one of DVSA's approved providers. There are about twenty-five of these located around the UK. The alternative is to take the three-part entrance examination administered by the DVSA. The format of this exam is very similar to the ADI qualifying process. In both instances there are fees to pay. If you take the fleet course route you will need to pay the provider's fee along with the DVSA registration fee, currently £120. If you take the examination route then you will need to pay for each test and, again, pay the DVSA registration fee. The fees are:

- Theory test   £66
- Driving ability test   £134.40
- Instructional ability test   £134.40

To find an accredited course or apply for the examination route, visit www.gov.uk. Further details about taking the accredited course or examination route are given in the DVSA publication *Your Guide to the Fleet Driver Trainers Register.* This can be found and downloaded as a PDF document from www.gov.uk

You can make a postcode search to locate the nearest provider. Make sure that the course provided suits all your requirements and needs, as well as budget, before you make any commitment.

Questions to consider are:

1. How long is the course?

2. How much time is spent on classroom and in-car training?

3. How many delegates will be participating?

4. How much pre-course theoretical preparation and study is there?

5. How will the course prepare you for the real world of corporate driving?

During the course, you should expect to learn about the fleet market and how you see yourself fitting into it, how best to present yourself and your product, as well as how to assess and identify training needs (ITN), how to coach, and how to give feedback to qualified drivers. The course should cover other important areas such as meeting clients, selling the benefits of your programme, checking driving licences, conducting vehicle safety checks, delivering a short occupational road risk presentation, developing commentary, and demonstration driving techniques.

"ROADCRAFT"

The essential source of reference for the delivery of advanced driving is the 1994 (or later) edition of *Roadcraft: The Police Driver's Handbook.* The training and development you deliver will need to be predominately in a coaching style, and should be based on the advice given in this publication.

As ADIs, we treat *Driving: The Essential Skills* as the official interpretation of the "Highway Code", but it's worth considering that *Roadcraft* pre-dates this considerably. Published in 1954 under the title *Attention All Drivers*, it was the first major driving technique publication in the UK, following the official Highway Code book, which was published in 1931. *Driving: The Ministry of Transport Manual* was not published until 1969.

The same team that published *Roadcraft* produced an excellent publication for corporate drivers titled *Fleetcraft: The Essential Occupational Driver's Handbook*. As well as dealing with the technical aspects of driving, it addresses company obligations under health and safety law in a simple and concise way. It is presently out of print, awaiting commercial sponsorship.

HACKNEY CARRIAGE & PRIVATE HIRE TAXIS

As an ADI, you are qualified to deliver driver training for taxi drivers. Each of the 400 or so local authorities has its own requirements regarding the issue of Hackney Carriage and Private Hire Vehicle licenses. Some councils require potential taxi drivers to pass a driving assessment, while others insist on them taking the DVSA taxi test.

In general, the other skills specific to taxi drivers that you would need to teach include a reversing manoeuvre, along with knowledge of where it's safe to stop/places where it's dangerous for passengers to alight the taxi. Drivers will need to be prepared for a few verbal questions on the "Highway Code", as well as being able to identify some traffic signs and road markings. For wheelchair-enhanced vehicles, the driver will need to demonstrate correct use of the equipment. Candidates taking a "black cab" style test will need to answer some related "cabology" questions. Examples of these include the dimensions of the taxi, its correct tyre pressures, and knowledge of what to do if a passenger leaves property behind.

EMERGENCY RESPONSE

Up until very recently, there was no formal requirement for people driving emergency response vehicles to be trained beyond an ordinary driving licence. However, the introduction of Section 19 to the Road Traffic Regulations Act 2006 is designed to ensure that any driver now working on behalf of the statutory emergency services is adequately trained to use the exemptions available. Now, an increasing number of ADIs provide training to the emergency services, including the blue-light element.

Emergency response driver training is delivered in-house or may be outsourced. It involves both classroom and on/off road practical elements. Instructors delivering this training typically come from the ranks of each service. In the instance of the ambulance service, the awarding body FutureQuals sets the standard of driver training under direction from the ambulance Driver Training and Advisory Group (DTAG).

LEVEL 4 DIPLOMA IN EMERGENCY RESPONSE AMBULANCE DRIVING INSTRUCTION QUALIFICATION (DERADI)

This course will cost in the region of £8,000 plus VAT. Guided Learning Hours account for 150 hours mentored training and 300 hours distant mentored training. The course typically takes 19 weeks. There are six mandatory units, which are divided into three sections:

- Seven weeks of training.

- Four weeks of supervised practice (instruction on a L3 CERAD Course).

- Eight weeks of consolidated practice.

The course prerequisites include the **Level 3 Certificate in Emergency Response Ambulance Driving (CERAD).** This is a course in ambulance driving, including emergency response, which costs in the region of £2,500 plus VAT. You also need to have:

1. Full UK driving licence for the C1 Licence Category for a minimum of 3 years.

2. No more than three penalty points.

3. Level 3 Certificate in Assessing Vocational Achievement (CAVA), to be completed before certification (must be working towards).

4. Level 4 Certificate in Education and Training (PTLLS, DTLLS, QTLLS) (or be working towards).

The content of this course focuses on:

- Enhanced knowledge, behaviours, understanding and skills required to instruct, coach, support, and assess learners in routine and emergency response ambulance demonstration driving.

- Knowledge and understanding of driving legislation, regulation, standards and agreed ways of working to ensure the driver is safe and competent as set out in the requirements stated in the High-Speed Driver Training Competencies.

- How human factors can influence attitude to risk.

It also covers the completion of the Ambulance Driver Risk Index [ADR], developing a working knowledge of the Goals for Driver Education [GDE] framework, and completion of the Driving Instructor Ambulance Driver Risk Index to measure progression and development.

Course providers include the St. John's Ambulance Service and private agencies such as EMSTAR (Emergency Services Training and Resilience); Elite Advanced Driver Training, and Frontline Training Services (FTS).

THE OFFICIAL REGISTER OF DRIVING INSTRUCTOR TRAINING (ORDIT)

"Train the trainer"—coaching and mentoring other ADIs.

ORDIT is a voluntary scheme run by the DVSA for those ADIs who wish to train new driving instructors. The law regulates driving instruction in a car, so this would only apply to training for Part 2 of the ADI examination.

You do not legally need an extra qualification to train driving instructors. To become an ORDIT trainer, you must:

1. Be an ADI.

2. Have achieved a Grade A for your latest ADI Standards Check (a Grade A in your ADI Part 3 test does not count).

You will then need to pass a practical assessment of your training skills with the DVSA.

The assessment lasts up to one hour and 30 minutes. This includes:

- A short time at the start, where the examiner will ask you about the trainee you've brought with you.

- Around one hour where you give a training session to your trainee.

- 15 minutes at the end where the examiner will give you your result and feedback.

You need to take:

- Your ADI certificate (badge).

- A suitable car (it must meet the same rules as cars used for the ADI Part 3 test).

- A trainee.

- Your trainee's ADI certificate or trainee instructor licence (this must be displayed in the windscreen if the trainee is paying you for the session).

- Training records for your trainee.

Your trainee must be either:

- Someone training to become an ADI.

- A qualified ADI.

During your assessment, your trainee can either:

- Train a real learner driver, while you give regular guidance and feedback from the back of the car.

- "Train" you if you are role-playing a learner and are simulating faults for them to correct.

You also need to bring either:

- A log of the training you have been doing with your trainee, if you have trained them before.

- An overview of how you intend to record your trainee's progress (for example, a blank template) if you have not trained them before.

- If your trainee is providing a lesson to a real learner driver, they need to bring training records for their learner.

Before the assessment, the examiner will ask you some questions about your trainee. You need to be able to tell them:

- What parts of the "National Standard for Driver and Rider Training" your trainee has covered so far.

- Your trainee's strengths and weaknesses.

- The training theme for the session.

The training themes include:

- Preparing to train learner drivers.

- Designing learning programmes.

- Enabling safe and responsible driving.

- Delivering driver training programmes.

- Managing risk to the instructor, learner, and third parties.

- Evaluating and developing knowledge, understanding and skills in the driver training industry.

Other training themes might also be appropriate, depending on your trainee.

During the assessment, the examiner will look for evidence that you meet the national standard for driver and rider training. You will be marked on 17 areas of competence. These are grouped into three categories:

- Trainer's lesson planning.

- Trainer's management of risk.

- Trainer's teaching and learning strategies.

You will get a score from 0 to 3 for each of the 17 competencies, which are added up to work out if you've passed the assessment. To pass, you need to score at least 43 out of 51.

After the assessment, the examiner will:

- Tell you the result of your assessment.

- Give you a copy of the ORDIT assessment report.

- Give you feedback on the assessment.

If you pass the assessment, you can register as an ORDIT trainer. If you fail your first attempt, then you can re-sit the assessment. However, you will have to book and pay again.

If you fail your second attempt, you will not qualify as an ORDIT trainer, but you can continue to be an ADI. The DVSA will write to you when you're next due to take an ADI Standards Check. You need to pass the check with a Grade A if you want to try again to qualify as a driving instructor trainer.

You can be removed from the ADI register if you do not book the standards check, or if you fail it.

The DVSA fees, including VAT for ORDIT, are currently subject to review:

Premises inspection:	£207.30
Trainer inspection:	£151.20
Final registration:	£120.00
Dual registrations:	£18.00

OTHER OPPORTUNITIES

You make your own good fortune. Participating in CPD, along with networking within this industry, can open doors. As well as changing and improving the way you teach, you can learn of other work opportunities, including working on international contracts.

JOIN A TRADE ASSOCIATION

Be part of the industry. You need to network with other people, as working alone is unlikely to help you learn of career changing opportunities. Trade association details can be found in Appendix 6, Networking Contacts.

APPENDIX 1

THE ELECTRIC REVOLUTION

The Future is Automatic

In our introduction to this book, we said that this is an exciting, indeed revolutionary time to join this industry. The biggest technological change since the invention of the internal combustion engine is here.

We have an unstoppable emergence of electric vehicles (EVs) on our roads. Driving schools of various sizes are beginning to choose electric tuition cars. 2030, when new petrol and diesel engines will be banned is not so far away. With the demise of the traditional engines, learners will no longer need to learn how to change gears and use the clutch. All electric vehicles are automatic, so they are much easier and safer to drive!

According to the DVSA, the proportion of learner drivers taking their test in an automatic rather than a manual car has more than tripled since 2008. Back in 2008, only 3.8% of tests were taken in an automatic vehicle, by the end of 2021 this has grown to 13.8%.

There are still some uncertainties about EVs such as their range before a re-charge, along with availability of charging points. There are government schemes to address such issues, including the fitting of home electric charging points. There are some 16,000 public fast charging points in the UK, the government pledges that no electric vehicle owner be more than 30 miles away from their nearest charging point by 2030. Make an internet search for "Zap Map" to check for updates.

EVs are very expensive to buy and insure, but as they become more mainstream costs will reduce. This will mean that they're more accessible for all drivers, including young drivers!

It almost goes without saying – electric cars are better for the environment. They emit fewer greenhouse gases and air pollutants over their life span. Even after the production of the vehicle and the generation of the electricity required to fuel them, opting for an EV is a potential way to cut vehicle running costs, as well as a contribution to improving the environment.

There is plenty of choice of EVs to suit your personal preferences. Trainers will need to shop around, the same as you would with a petrol or diesel car. Driver trainers will also need to adapt to "teach electric". Changes to the teaching content will include regenerative braking – a different feel for the accelerator; no gears or clutch, even driving with one pedal, conserving battery power, how and where to charge an EV etc, etc.

TEACH ELECTRIC

Electric cars are "automatic". You have two pedals only, accelerator and footbrake. Simple, and arguably safer to drive because you can focus more on the road and traffic ahead.

Because an electric car doesn't need a clutch, it also doesn't require gears. Electric vehicles don't feature a multi-speed gearbox like petrol or diesel vehicles. Instead, they have just one gear. This is because they can achieve much higher engine revs than a conventional fuel engine. Internal combustion engines reach around 4,000-6,000 revs per minute (rpm), whereas an electric motor can achieve up to 20,000 rpm. This doesn't mean that electric cars can't have gears, but they aren't necessary to make the car run.

Aside from adapting to teach an automatic car, regenerative braking is the biggest technical change the driver trainer should face. You can expect this kind of braking to have a detrimental effect on brake pedal feel, it can take some time to get used to this.

When decelerating or braking, the lost (kinetic) energy is used to recharge the car's batteries. To varying degrees, this can affect the feel for the car when slowing. With some cars, the regenerative force isn't very strong. It can feel a bit like being in a high gear and using engine braking to slow down in a petrol or diesel car.

Regenerative braking systems are already used on many modern cars. When driving these cars, the system is virtually imperceptible to the driver. However, when driving hybrid or pure electric cars, regenerative braking takes a more active and obvious role. Brake regeneration helps to charge the larger batteries that directly drive the car. When you lift your foot off the accelerator pedal and onto the brake, the system starts to put energy back into the battery. You can feel the car start to slow down. The sensation will feel different, depending on the car manufacturer. Some tailor the way it feels to your own preference. To harvest as much wasted energy, it can be possible to choose the maximum setting, or if you dislike the sensation of the car braking itself, you can turn it off.

One pedal driving is where you can use the accelerator pedal to completely control the car's speed. Taking your foot off the gas pedal completely will feel like you've got your foot firmly on the brake. Drivers need to modulate the right foot to speed up and slow down, rather than swapping between the brake and accelerator pedals.

You can expect the brake lights to come on if the car is slowing quickly, even if you're not even touching the brake pedal.

The future of motoring is electric. This revolution makes this a "must have" CPD for all ADIs!

APPENDIX 2

THE SMITH SYSTEM

Good Driving Habits

So, we are looking for a way to teach driving in a positive "goal-based" way, avoiding the negativity of fault-based instruction. The question is, does the Smith System work for you?

WHAT ARE THE ORIGINS OF THE SMITH SYSTEM?

Since the police began keeping records of traffic collisions in 1926, their investigations have always focused on what caused the crash, with most collisions being attributed to driver error rather than a mechanical fault. However, in the 1950s, three American researchers took a different approach—by looking at how good drivers avoided collisions. The three researchers were Harold A. Smith, John J. Cummings, and Reuel A. Sherman. Smith was a professional driving instructor who worked for the Ford Motor Company in its fleet driving division, whilst Cummings was a traffic collision investigator and Sherman was a recognised authority on occupational vision.

From this work, they devised a visual search method that took the form of "five seeing habits". The concept behind the Smith System is principally one of having a "space cushion". This can easily be achieved by driving at an appropriate speed for the road and traffic conditions—that is, by being able to stop well within a safe distance, and having space and time to evaluate hazards as and when they arise, instead of having to react suddenly. The outcome will be a defensive driving style that is smooth, progressive, unobtrusive and above all, safe. And ultimately, that's what every driver should be aiming for.

FIVE SEEING HABITS

Driving is essentially about changing our vehicle's speed and/or direction. The critical abilities needed for this are: attention, perception, judgement/planning ability, and having enough time to react safely.

The following seeing habits are designed to help new drivers and their trainers achieve this:

1. **Look well ahead.** Aim high to steer—search 20-30 seconds ahead, not just down at the vehicle in front.

2. **Spot the problems**. Get the big picture—look out for all other hazards such as car doors opening and pedestrians stepping out from between parked vehicles. Expect the unexpected.

3. **Move your eyes**. Keep your eyes moving—use your mirrors, avoid the fixed stare, and use your peripheral vision.

4. **Keep space**. Apply your separation distance and have an escape route—anticipate an emergency situation developing.

5. **Be seen**. Make sure other road users see you—using eye contact, direction/brake lights, headlight signals, or the horn.

The Smith System is a very simple and easily understandable way to teach and learn. Its concepts have been used and developed worldwide by driver trainers, particularly in the United States and Canada.

Most crashes are preventable, providing that the right driving habits are learned, practiced, and applied consistently. The development of its interlocking good habits, combined with the advice, guidance and law provided in our Highway Code combines to make a great package.

At the very least it provides UK driver trainers with another tool to choose when delivering driver training.

APPENDIX 3

EVALUATING YOUR OWN DRIVING

Are you a really a good driver?

How well are you doing?

It's important to understand that how **you** drive will have a significant bearing on what you teach your learners. In this chapter, we're going to test that. Take a look below, and answer the following questions with "Always" "Sometimes" or "Never".

Before you start driving, do you...

1. Make sure you are wearing sensible footwear?

2. Follow the advice given in the "Highway Code" about vehicle checks?

3. Follow the advice given in "Driving – Essential Skills" about checking your brakes?

4. Do your "Cockpit Drill"? Are you sure that your deportment behind the steering wheel is correct?

5. Check that your handbrake is applied and that your gear lever is in neutral?

If you always do all five—well done! Now, spend 15 to 20 minutes on the next 100 evaluation questions. Just like before, answer with "Always", "Sometimes" or "Never".

Do you:

1. Drive when you are tired?

2. Drive when you feel unwell?

3. Drive when you feel upset?

4. Forget to "find the biting point" before moving off uphill?

5. Forget to use "brake control" when preparing to move off downhill?

6. Forget to look over your right shoulder before moving off from the nearside kerb edge?

7. Signal before looking in the mirrors or over your right shoulder?

8. Take your hand off the steering wheel in order to operate the direction indicator?

9. Forget to cancel a left turn signal before moving off?

10. Forget to cancel a left turn signal when leaving a roundabout?

11. Rest your left hand on the gear lever, at the same time as keeping your right hand at the bottom of the steering wheel?

12. Slouch in the driving seat?

13. Rest your right elbow on the door ledge?

14. Cross your arms when steering?

15. Allow the steering wheel to spin back after a turn?

16. Steer in a short and shuffling manner?

17. Allow either hand to pass over the twelve o'clock or six o'clock position?

18. Turn the steering wheels while stationary?

19. Rest the palm(s) of your hand(s) on the steering wheel?

20. Allow your fingers to fidget on the steering wheel?

21. Steer too quickly or early to the left after an overtake?

22. Smoke cigarettes or vape when driving?

23. Let your eyes hold their attention too long in the wrong place(s)?

24. Turn your head to talk to your passenger(s)?

25. Signal and then check in the mirrors as you approach a turn?

26. Begin to change direction before using the mirrors?

27. Signal unnecessarily when passing parked vehicles?

28. Signal to the left after an overtake on a two-way road?

29. Give "arm signals" with one finger?

30. Move your head to check your interior mirror?

31. Look over your right hand shoulder while turning right, changing lane or overtaking?

32. Look over your left hand shoulder before turning left, changing lane, or completing an overtake?

33. Believe that you can "check the mirrors" without moving your eyes?

34. Believe that your peripheral vision is adequate for knowing what is following or to your side?

35. Race the engine when changing gears?

36. Change gear with an open left hand (palm)?

37. Change gear too hurriedly with jerky movements?

38. Change gear in the middle of an overtake?

39. Forget which gear you are driving in?

40. Glance at the gear lever to check which gear you are in?

41. Put your left hand on the gear lever and declutch in preparation for a gear change, and find that you are already in the gear you were going to change to?

42. Change up through the gears too early?

43. Stay in a lower gear for a needlessly long time?

44. Forget to change down gear before a hill where necessary?

45. Forget to change down gear before a bend where necessary?

46. Forget to change up after a hazard?

47. When slowing down, change down through the gears, one by one?

48. Change gear when turning a corner?

49. Rest (ride) your left foot on the clutch?

50. Slip the clutch in second gear at extremely low speeds?

51. Leave your braking to the last moment, and find yourself braking hard?

52. Use your driving mirrors after you have started to slow down?

53. Simultaneously push the clutch and brake down together when stopping?

54. Coast to a stop by selecting neutral on the approach to a red traffic signal?

55. Apply the handbrake without pushing in the ratchet button?

56. Begin to apply the handbrake before your car has stopped?

57. Forget to apply the handbrake in circumstances where you are likely to have to wait for some time?

58. Hold the handbrake in the "off" position while waiting to proceed?

59. Take chances, rather than safe opportunities? For instance, when emerging at road junctions.

60. When emerging on a right turn at a T-junction where the visibility is poor, steer to the right too soon?

61. Loiter unnecessarily, like a learner driver at hazards?

62. Fail to make progress where safe?

63. In slow moving traffic, pull up less than half a car length from the next vehicle in front of you?

64. Get caught behind a service bus pulling up to allow passengers to alight?

65. Drive too fast for the road and traffic conditions?

66. Have to keep checking your speedometer in an attempt to avoid driving over the speed limit?

67. Become overfamiliar with local knowledge?

68. Find unfamiliar roads difficult to negotiate?

69. Take corners so fast that you find yourself trying to brake, change gear, declutch, and steer at the same time?

70. Cut right-hand corners?

71. Allow your offside wheels to cross the centre line of the road when turning right?

72. Position too wide when turning left?

73. Position too close to the left when turning right?

74. Drive unnecessarily close to the centre of a two way road?

75. Drive too close to the left/parked vehicles?

76. Drive in the centre lane of a motorway, when the left-hand lane is clear of traffic?

77. Forget to give pedal cyclists and horse riders plenty of room before and when overtaking?

78. Overtake a vehicle ahead, when you can see there is traffic closely or quickly approaching from the opposite direction?

79. Use the horn as a rebuke to other road users?

80. Wait at red traffic lights in first gear with the handbrake released, ready to move off on the red and amber signals?

81. Accelerate unnecessarily through a large, open, and busy roundabout?

82. When approaching a quiet roundabout, stop when you could have kept going?

83. When approaching a quiet roundabout behind another motor car, anticipate the driver proceeding, only to realise that he or she stops unnecessarily?

84. Accelerate out of a roundabout before your car is on a straight course?

85. Signal to the right when proceeding "straight ahead" at a roundabout?

86. Forget to signal to the right, when turning right at a roundabout?

87. When leaving a roundabout which has been built over or under a dual carriageway, signal to the left as you pass the last remaining entrance to the roundabout before your exit road?

88. Overtake articulated lorries or buses on roundabouts?

89. Overtake "three abreast"?

90. Overtake in situations contrary to the advice given in the "Highway Code"?

91. Tuck in very close to a large vehicle in front, before attempting to overtake?

92. Allow your driving to slow down unnecessarily when giving "running commentaries"?

93. When leaving a motorway, reduce your speed on the main carriageway?

94. Park your car on the pavement?

95. Park on a single or double yellow/red line(s)?

96. Double park, or conceal an entrance or traffic sign?

97. Turn the car round by means of forward and reverse gears in more than three "points" in a wide road?

98. Continuously use your interior mirror to check the road is clear behind, whilst you reverse and steer round corners using the palm of your right hand on the steering wheel?

99. Get annoyed with the antics of some drivers and flash your headlights at any driver who makes a mistake?

100. Blame your mistakes on the car you are driving/being nervous/under supervision /not being familiar with the roads?

Hopefully your answers here were mostly "never". But, of course, nobody is perfect. Even the very best trainers make mistakes from time to time, so don't be too hard on yourself if you haven't achieved 100 out of 100.

Now, have a go at the final exercise, again answering with "Always", "Sometimes" and "Never".

Do you:

1. Look well ahead and plan your driving in advance?

2. Concentrate fully on your driving?

3. Drive with responsibility, taking into full account the likely actions of all other road users?

4. Use your experience to accurately time your actions to fit in safely with all other road users?

5. Keep your eyes moving?

6. Avoid focusing your attention on "distractions"?

7. Have an "escape route"?

8. Give "running commentaries"?

9. Use your car's controls smoothly?

10. Use acceleration sense on approach to hazards, thereby minimising the use of the brake?

11. Feed the steering wheel through your hands using the "pull-push" system?

12. Keep your thumbs on the inner rim, not locked round the wheel?

13. Keep your fingers wrapped lightly round the wheel?

14. Hold the gear lever knob in the palm of your closed left hand, tilted to the left or right, where this is helpful?

15. Move off on an uphill gradient without rolling back?

16. Use brake control when moving off downhill?

17. Follow the advice given in the "Highway Code" in respect to your use of speed?

18. Gauge your use of speed with focal points in the road ahead?

19. Gauge your position by using focal points?

20. Anticipate green traffic lights or pelican/puffin lights changing, and progressively slow down on the approach?

21. Slow down progressively on approach to a blind bend, humpback bridge, brow of a hill, and unmarked crossroads?

22. Consider the dangers of a rural road without a pavement?

23. Check the condition of the road surface?

24. Check the outside mirrors well before direction changes on fast roads, roundabouts, or in slow traffic queues?

25. Keep within the recommended following distances given in the "Highway Code"?

26. Increase your following distance when the road surface is wet or icy?

27. Use building lines and breaks for information of a possible danger ahead?

28. Open the window in foggy conditions to listen for traffic approaching?

29. Look out for motorcyclists well before emerging at a junction?

30. When proceeding at crossroads where you have priority, check for danger from both sides?

31. Give way to a driver waiting to emerge from a junction on your left, when you are in a line of slow-moving traffic?

32. Before turning into or out of a junction, look and check for pedestrians nearby?

33. Continuously reassess the prevailing traffic conditions whilst waiting at red traffic light signals?

34. Respond sufficiently early to all traffic signs, lights, and road markings?

35. Leave enough room when passing parked vehicles?

36. Wait and let approaching vehicles through, where the width of the road is narrowed by parked cars on both sides?

37. Overtake only when safe, that is, with an adequate safety margin ahead and behind?

38. Consider a slowing down arm signal when approaching a zebra crossing where pedestrians are waiting?

39. Let pedestrians continue a sufficient distance across a pedestrian crossing before moving off?

40. Stop before a junction when an LGV or PCV is turning into the narrow road that you are on?

41. Switch your front and/or rear fog lamps only when visibility is really bad (i.e. less than 100 metres)?

42. Switch your lights on when using a multi-storey car park?

43. Look over your left shoulder whilst straight reversing?

44. Keep your car within one and a half feet (45cm) of the kerb when reversing?

45. Consider sensible use of the horn when approaching a hazard?

46. Consider flashing the headlamps before overtaking?

47. Look fully round the outside of the car before beginning to steer or change the lock on a "set piece" manoeuvre?

48. Show awareness of the camber effects on corners and bends?

49. Bring your car to a smooth and comfortable "chauffeur driver's" stop?

50. Apply a high level of competence?

Hopefully, your answers here were mostly "always"!

Having completed these three exercises, reflect on what is best practice when teaching learner drivers. Discuss your thoughts with your trainer.

APPENDIX 4

MIND MAPS

Organise your thinking

Visual Key Points

A "mind map" is a self-drawn diagram used to visually organise information. You can do this on your own, or by "brainstorming" with a team of people.

Mind mapping helps you to collect information and create ideas for any subject or topic you like. Most likely, it will make you a better thinker! Mind maps can be used to help you plan your driving lesson to suit an individual learner.

HOW TO DO THIS?

A central theme is placed in the centre of a blank piece of paper. This is the title, the subject, a problem, or just a thought. In our examples we have chosen "Positive Driving: Good Habits", "Negative Driving: Dislikes" and "Anticipation". Following these examples, you can create your own for other lesson topics or areas. Start with our "SOAP" style lesson plans in Chapter 9.

Cat B License acquisition		Post Cat B License acquisition
• Explanation of the Controls • Moving Away and Making • Normal Stops • Use of Mirrors • Use of Signals • Emergency Stop • Approaching Junctions: Major to • Minor • Approaching Junctions: Minor to • Major • Crossroads • Roundabouts • Pedestrian Crossings • Awareness and Anticipation	• Judgement when Meeting & • Crossing approaching Traffic; • Overtaking • Keep Space: Clearances & • Following Distances • Use of Speed & Making Progress • Road Positioning • Eco-Safe Driving • Independent Driving • Traffic Signs, Signals and Road • Markings • Satellite Navigation • Reversing • Bay Parking	• Town Driving • All Weather Driving • Out of Town Driving and Rural • Roads • Night Driving • Dual Carriageway Driving • Motorway Driving • Advanced Driving • Corporate Driver Development • Car Towing • Large Goods Vehicle • Passenger Carrying Vehicle

1. **POSITIVE DRIVING: Good driving habits**

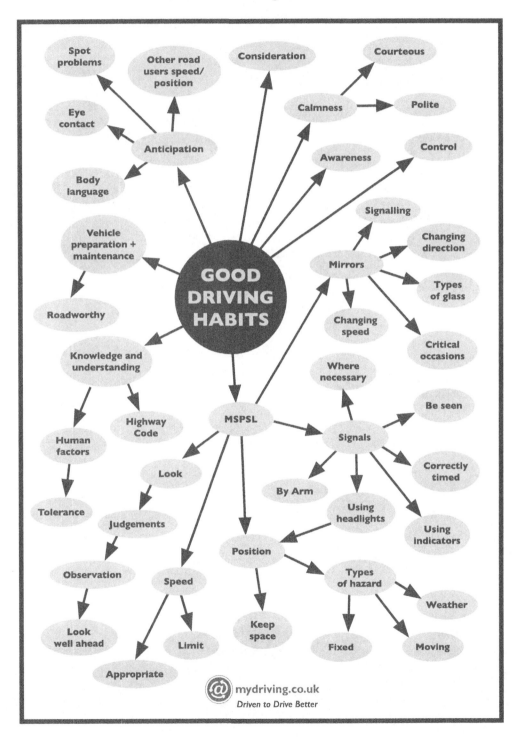

2. NEGATIVE DRIVING: Dislikes about driving

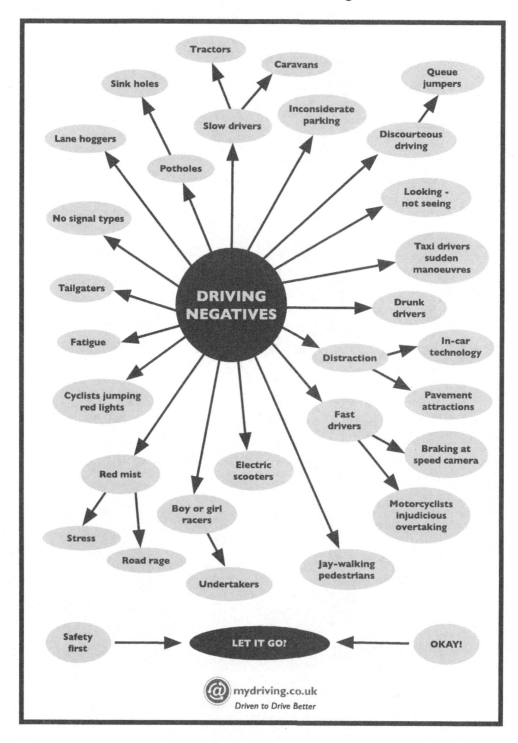

3. ANTICIPATION: Forward Planning

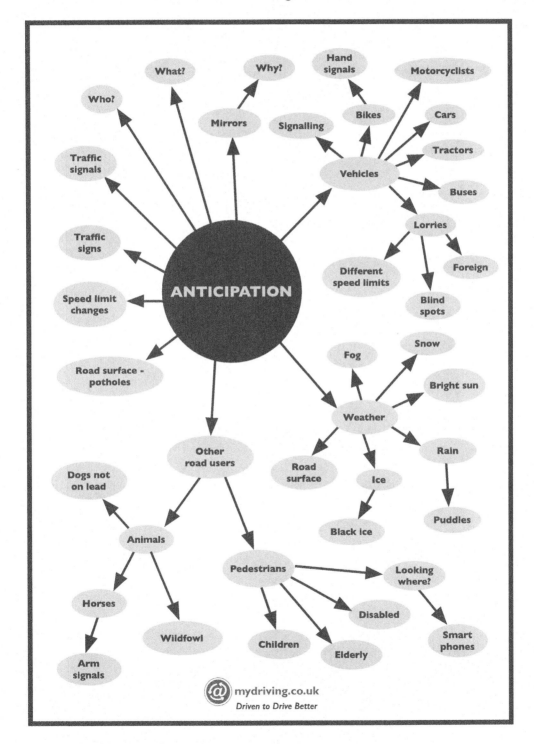

APPENDIX 5

CAUSES OF ROAD
TRAFFIC COLLISIONS

It's about behaviour

The first fatal traffic collision in Britain was on 17th August 1896, in Crystal Palace, Southeast London. The victim was a pedestrian—Bridget Driscoll—who was knocked down and killed by a motorised carriage. A new era of transport and danger was upon us.

Just three years later, the next serious collision hit the headlines. This time it involved the car's occupants being killed. On 23rd February 1899, Harrow on the Hill in Northwest London, a driver was attempting to turn a corner at over 25mph when one of the car's rear wheels collapsed and the vehicle hit a brick wall. The occupants were thrown out, and the driver and front seat passenger killed. A roadside plaque records this incident, and the newspapers at the time expressed hope that this terrible road accident would "convince drivers to take greater care and keep their speed down". Unfortunately, the plaque did not work! As well as lives lost and life-changing injuries, road traffic collisions today cost the UK economy more than £16.5 billion per year.

ROAD CASUALTIES

Road casualty statistics boast that despite more cars, buses, lorries, motorcycles, and bicycles flowing onto our roads each year, the UK's roads have remained amongst the safest not only in Europe, but the world. With improved vehicle safety features, tighter traffic regulations, as well as greater public awareness, serious collisions **are** on the decline. In addition, government figures from 2019 report that "casualties of all severities" were 5% lower than in 2018; this is the lowest level since 1979 when this statistical series with current definitions and detail began.

Of course, in the real world we know that driving is not without its perils. Dash cam footage on social media records enormous numbers of crashes, near misses, and examples of bad driving manners. In fact, these dash cam videos are now being used by the police to enforce laws and regulations and help to deter poor and dangerous driving. DVLA data reveals that more than three million driving licence holders have penalty points on their licences, and that around 100,000 drivers have been disqualified over the past four years alone, for reaching twelve penalty points. What does this reflect?

BAD DRIVING CAUSES CRASHES

For a significant minority of drivers, politeness and courtesy are replaced with selfishness and aggression. This is epitomised by the madcap motoring animation released by Walt Disney Productions in 1950, "Motor Mania". Goofy is a Mr. Hyde-type split personality. The pleasant, friendly, and good-natured "Mr. Walker" who "wouldn't hurt a fly nor step on an ant", undergoes a change in personality to become the mean, reckless, and predatory "Mr. Wheeler" when he gets behind the wheel of his car.

Likewise, one of the most-watched factual series on UK television is "Traffic Cops". This series, amongst others, depicts work of police traffic officers dealing with misdemeaning drivers. Bad driving makes good television!

BEHAVIOUR BREEDS BEHAVIOUR

A study by the London School of Economics (LSE) and the tyre manufacturer Goodyear, found that drivers' choices of behaviour on the road trigger what is described as a "ripple effect". In a survey of nearly 9,000 drivers from 15 European countries, 87% of those surveyed agreed that considerate driving by others can prompt them, in turn, to be considerate to other drivers. Conversely, 55% admitted that when irritated or provoked on the road by one driver, they may be more likely to take it out on another. The report suggests that a "simple act of kindness or one of aggression can initiate a chain of events creating an environment that is either comfortable and safer, or stressful and more dangerous for drivers."

YOUNG DRIVERS

Young, inexperienced drivers are often labelled careless and reckless. However, it is far too easy to place blame on just a select group of road users, as drivers can form bad habits long after passing their driving test. As driver trainers, we have a considerable influence on new drivers. By utilising the GDE matrix and other evidenced information, we are in a key position to help turn around the statistical fact that inexperienced young drivers are disproportionately likely to be involved in crashes.

Collisions happen every day, and they are avoidable:

1. Being Careless, Inconsiderate or in a Hurry

The influence and pressures of everyday living can lead to motoring accidents. We live in a fast-moving world; such are our expectations of an "on demand society". So, when people drive, they are often in a hurry and stressed. It is an understandable situation, and something that most people will be able to relate to.

Many collisions are caused by driving too fast for the conditions. This is not to be confused with speeding (though this is sometimes a factor); it means making traffic manoeuvres without slowing down to a safe speed, such as anticipating other traffic correctly, taking a bend in the road or changing lanes, or being aware of road and weather conditions.

Bad weather conditions such as ice, hail, snow, and bright sunshine aggravate the circumstances. Driving at speed during heavy rainfall may cause a car to "aquaplane"— this is where the tyres lose grip and traction on the road's surface water, causing the driver to lose control.

Another outcome of driving in a hurried state, and one which is much too common, is driving too close to the vehicle in front. This is often referred to as "tailgating". Statistically, the most common collision is the rear end shunt.

2. Failing to Judge Another Person's Path and/or Speed

This can be associated with "being careless, inconsiderate or in a hurry". The Highway Code provides simple advice: "Wait until there is a safe gap between you and any oncoming vehicle".

The most common officially recorded reason for crashes is "failing to look properly". For instance, misjudging a gap when pulling out of a junction, or when attempting to negotiate a busy roundabout. Another is wrongly assuming that another vehicle will make the manoeuvre that you expect them to make.

Ultimately, it is human nature for people to take risks, usually based on experience (or lack of it) and making assumptions. But, when the margins are so fine, the odds for dangerous and tragic consequences are that much higher and beyond reasonable expectations.

3. **Distracted and Complacent Drivers**

Judgement is likely to be impaired by distractions whilst driving, perhaps by a fellow passenger, peer pressure, a mobile device or the radio, or even other things going on outside the vehicle, but not in front of you. Keeping your eyes and concentration on the road ahead is key to a driver's safety.

Some collisions may be caused by driver complacency, familiarity with the route, or even laziness. We need to drive "on sight", not on memory of what we expect to be there. Again, making assumptions is a dangerous game to play. Anticipation is an important skill to employ when behind the wheel of a car, and is a central tenant of "defensive driving". Its outcome is an informed and calculated reaction to developing on-road circumstances—expect the unexpected!

Of course, it goes without saying that mobile phones are a major distraction whilst driving. Despite the increased penalties and warnings (currently six points on your licence and a £200 fine), they have become the backbone of our lives professionally and privately. It makes them difficult to ignore for most people, and blinds them to the very real dangers they present when behind the wheel. Is a small fine and a few points on a driving licence a good enough deterrent to reduce the number of drivers using their mobile phones?

It's important that we can drive "on sight", not on memory of what we expect to be there. Driving is probably the most dangerous activity any of us will do in our lives; it always requires and demands full attention.

4. **Poor Health, Stress and Fatigue, Alcohol, and Drug Use**

Government targets for reducing traffic collisions in recent times have largely focused on engineering and technological advancements. Human factors such as stress and psychological states, sleep, fatigue, and alertness, as well as general health status of drivers, have gained more attention in recent years. These aspects can be reviewed and researched within the "Lifestyle" aspect of the GDE matrix.

For many years, drink driving has been one of the most highly publicised causes of road collisions. This issue has not gone away. It may seem that the obvious is being stated, but it still seems that drivers need to be reminded to plan their journeys—if they intend to drink, they must make alternative travel arrangements for the return trip with a colleague or friend, or use a taxi. If the drink is spontaneous, then they must stay within limits or seek a lift home. Alcohol is for recreational purposes only, so it is relatively simple to abstain or monitor your intake. Drug driving is more complex, as legislation, drugs tests and police training are less well-established. However, the ability to detect, arrest, and prosecute offenders is now available; more police forces are becoming proactive in this respect.

Once again, these are aspects that can be reviewed and researched within the "Lifestyle" aspect of the GDE matrix.

Ultimately, it is essential that learners understand that learning to drive is more than just learning the mechanical skills needed to operate a car; attitude behind the wheel is the most important lesson to learn, and one which will keep them and all other road users safe. It is also the most important area of teaching we are charged with providing. A driver's mind, as well as the car, has to be in the correct gear!

APPENDIX 6

NETWORKING CONTACTS

You are not alone

This is a list of the organisations that are mostly likely to assist you in various ways in your new career as a driver trainer. Begin here, to network with the key players in this industry.

For details of commercial organisations and suppliers, we recommend that you contact one or more of the driving school associations. Look at their websites and ask them to send you a complimentary (electronic or hard) copy of their latest magazine.

1. DRIVER AND VEHICLE STANDARDS AGENCY (DVSA)

The Driver and Vehicle Standards Agency (DVSA) is a government agency. As an Executive Agency within the Department for Transport, the DVSA is the main regulatory body for driver training. It is responsible for setting standards for drivers, riders, and trainers by testing new drivers and riders fairly and efficiently.

The DVSA maintains the Registers of Approved Driving Instructors; Large Goods Vehicle Instructors; Fleet Trainers; Driving Instructor Trainers, and Post-Test Motorcycle Trainers. It also supervises Compulsory Basic Training (CBT) for learner motorcyclists, driver education, and the provision of learning resources, whilst ensuring that vehicle operators and MOT garages understand and follow roadworthiness standards.

Driver and Vehicle Standards Agency
The Axis Building
112 Upper Parliament Street
Nottingham, NG1 8LP

0300 790 6801
CustomerServices@dvsa.gov.uk
www.gov.uk

2. MOTOR SCHOOLS ASSOCIATION (MSA)

The Motor Schools Association of Great Britain is the senior national association for ADIs formed on March 31, 1935, just before the driving test was introduced.

The association's principal aims, then as now, are to keep members informed of any matters of interest to them, to represent the views of members to government, its departments, and agencies, to provide services that will be of benefit to members, and to set standards of professional and ethical behaviour for teachers of driving.

Motor Schools Association
4 Victoria Square, St Albans, Hertfordshire, AL1 3TF

01625 664501
mail@msagb.co.uk
www.msagb.com
Magazine: Newslink

3. DRIVING INSTRUCTORS ASSOCIATION (DIA)

The Driving Instructors Association (DIA) is the largest professional membership body for driver and rider trainers in the UK.

The DIA offers support, advice, and member benefits including £25m of professional indemnity and public liability insurance, legal assistance, and an ADI helpdesk to offer advice for driver trainers, as well as a monthly magazine and free webinars. Membership also includes discounts on goods and services for your home and business, as well as a range of other bonuses.

Driving Instructors Association
11 Gleneagles Court
Brighton Road
Crawley RH10 6AD

020 8686 8010
dia@driving.org
www.driving.org
Magazine: Driver Trainer

4. APPROVED DRIVING INSTRUCTORS NATIONAL JOINT COUNCIL (ADINJC)

Established in 1973, the ADINJC is one of the leading National Driving Instructor Associations in the UK. While the organisation is known as "the Association of Associations", driver trainers can join as individual members. The ADINJC is a non-profit making organisation. All income, after deductions for normal operating expenses, is devoted to activities to further enhance the opportunities and profitability of members.

ADI National Joint Council
16 Grosvenor Close,
Lichfield,
Staffordshire, WS14 9SR

0800 8202 444
membership@adinjc.org.uk
www.adinjc.org.uk
Ezine: ADINJC Members News

5. NATIONAL ASSOCIATIONS STRATEGIC PARTNERSHIP (NASP)

This is the steering group for the National Approved Driving Instructor Associations.

Formed in 2014, NASP represents the three main membership associations for driver trainers listed above, representing more than 20,000 driver and rider trainers.

www.n-a-s-p.co.uk

6. INSTITUTE OF MASTER TUTORS OF DRIVING (IMTD)

The IMTD is a small but well-respected, "behind the scenes" organisation, providing membership to some of the most experienced, highly qualified, and successful road safety practitioners and Approved Driving Instructors in the UK and Ireland. IMTD is a not-for-profit organisation, that keeps its members informed about the latest developments and technology in road safety and driver training. It also affords the opportunity to add credible post nominals to your name and use the institute insignia on stationery and other promotional materials.

Institute of Master Tutors of Driving (IMTD)
07748 303 545
secretary@imtd.org.uk
www.imtd.org.uk

7. THE GRAHAM FEEST CONSULTANCY

The Graham Feest Consultancy has been available now for several years, providing support and guidance to established driver trainers or those seeking to join the industry on non-technical matters of teaching people to drive. Setting up a driving school and understanding the overall contribution which the industry can and should be making to road safety are key elements when it comes to delivering safe drivers for the future. The Graham Feest Consultancy can make a difference to the approach which you should be making, and ensuring that your principles and ethos delivers in the right way.

Those entering the profession, as well as established trainers, are well-advised to contact Graham Feest for an initial chat. This service is offered free of charge.

graham@grahamfeest.com
www.grahamfeest.com
Ezine: Traffic Safety Roads

8. IAM ROADSMART

IAM RoadSmart, formerly called the Institute of Advanced Motorists, is a charity based in Chiswick, West London.

Originally formed in 1956, the organisation has more than two hundred voluntary affiliated groups around the country. Individual members of these groups have taken and passed the advanced test, and often make themselves available to help others do the same.

1 Albany Place
Hyde Way
Welwyn Garden City
Hertfordshire AL7 3BT

0300 303 1134
roadsmart@iam.org.uk
www.iamroadsmart.com
Magazine: *RoadSmart*

9. ROYAL SOCIETY FOR THE PREVENTION OF ACCIDENTS (ROSPA)

RoSPA's Advanced Drivers and Riders Association is a charity based in Birmingham.

The organisation originated in 1955 as the Finchley League of Safe Drivers. Today, the association has a network of over 50 local groups around the UK. These groups have trained and experienced tutors willing to offer free advice, assessments, and support to help drivers and motorcyclists prepare for their Advanced Driving/Motorcycling test.

Royal Society for the Prevention of Accidents
28 Calthorpe House
Edgbaston
Birmingham, B15 1RP

0121 248 2099
furtherinfo@roadar.org

www.roadar.org.uk
Magazine: *Care on the Road*

10. BRAKE, THE ROAD SAFETY CHARITY

"Brake" is a road safety charity that was founded in 1995.

Every 30 seconds, someone, somewhere in the world, is killed in a road crash. The misery of road deaths and injuries is a shameful epidemic that must end. "Brake" campaigns to stop the carnage and supports the victims.

Brake
PO Box 548 Huddersfield
West Yorkshire, HD1 2XZ

0808 8000 401
admin@brake.org.uk
www.brake.org.uk

11. NDORS: NATIONAL DRIVER OFFENDERS RETRAINING SCHEME

NDORS is for a motorist who has been caught committing what's known as a low-level traffic offence. They must attend a course focusing on re-education. The alternative is that the motorist has to pay a fine and have penalty points on their licence.

www.ukroed.org.uk

12. ARRM: THE ASSOCIATION FOR ROAD RISK MANAGEMENT

ARRM is the essential membership organisation for professionals and organisations involved in work-related road safety and the management of occupational road risk, collaborating with other organisations to promote innovation and share best practice.

White House,
Pagham Road, Lagness
Chichester PO20 1LN

www.arrm.org.uk

13. NPCC: NATIONAL POLICE CHIEF COUNCIL

The NPCC brings police forces in the UK together to help policing coordinate operations, reform, improve, and provide value for money. It was formed on April 1st, 2015, and replaced the Association of Chief Police Officers (ACPO). The NPCC continues to provide national police coordination and leadership.

www.npcc.police.uk

14. PACTS: Parliamentary Advisory Council for Transport Safety

PACTS's aim is to advise and inform members of the House of Commons and of the House of Lords on air, rail, and road safety issues. It brings together safety professionals and legislators to identify research-based solutions to transport safety problems.

www.pacts.org.uk

15. ROAD SAFETY FOUNDATION

The Road Safety Foundation conducts simultaneous action on all three components of the safe road system: roads, vehicles, and behaviour. Their activity in the last decade has concentrated on the European Road Assessment Programme (EuroRAP) in the UK and internationally.

www.roadsafetyfoundation.org

16. ROAD SAFETY GB

Road Safety GB is a national road safety organisation that includes representatives from groups across the UK, such as local government road safety teams. It works to develop a range of educational initiatives and to encourage the national debate on road safety.

www.roadsafetygb.org.uk

17. ROAD SAFETY SCOTLAND

Road Safety Scotland is part of Transport Scotland, the Scottish Government's transport agency. It works to promote awareness of road safety issues in Scotland and to ensure effective co-operation and communication between relevant bodies.

www.roadsafety.scot

18. ROAD SAFETY WALES

Road Safety Wales has been established to create "unity from diversity", by developing and sustaining co-operation and interaction between all key partners across Wales and/or agencies with the responsibility for road safety promotion.

www.roadsafetywales.org.uk

19. ROADSAFE

RoadSafe is a charitable partnership which brings together the private sector with government and road safety professionals by means of introducing representatives from government, the vehicle and component manufacturing, insurance and road transport industries, road safety professionals, and specialist media.

www.roadsafe.com

20. THINK!

THINK! provides road safety information for road users. The aim is to encourage safer behaviour and reduce the number of people killed and injured on our roads every year. They are also responsible for spearheading the government's road safety publicity campaign.

www.think.gov.uk

21. TRL: TRANSPORT RESEARCH LABORATORY

TRL works with governments, international funding institutions, and private sector clients to bring knowledge and understanding based on research and testing to a vast array of transport related issues. Established in 1933 and then privatised in 1996.

www.trl.co.uk

22. RHA: ROAD HAULAGE ASSOCIATION

The RHA is a membership organisation for the operators of commercial goods-carrying vehicles over 3.5 tonnes, freight clearing houses, trailer operators, recovery operators, and van operators.

www.rha.uk.net

23. DISABILITY DRIVING INSTRUCTORS

The Association of Disability Driving Instructors seeks to help people with physical disabilities, special educational needs, and those with hearing difficulties.

Disability Driving Instructors are an independent, not-for-profit Community Interest Company (CIC) set up in partnership with the Forum of Mobility

Centres (now Driving Mobility). They provide a "one stop shop" to help disabled people get impartial advice about how to start to learn to drive, how to return to driving after an incident or illness, and how to keep driving safely.

Disability Driving Instructors
Laburnum Cottage
Bennetts Lane, Crich, DE4 5BS

0844 800 7355
admin@disabilitydrivinginstructors.com
www.disabilitydrivinginstructors.com

24. QUEEN ELIZABETH FOUNDATION FOR DISABLED PEOPLE

The origins of QEF can be traced back as far as 1932. Today it is a leading disability charity, working with people that have physical and learning disabilities, or brain injuries, to help them gain new skills and increase independence for life.

Queen Elizabeth's Foundation for Disabled People
Leatherhead Court
Woodlands Road
Leatherhead
Surrey
KT22 0BN

Tel: 01372 841100
info@qef.org.uk
www.qef.org.uk

APPENDIX 7

LEARNING RESOURCES

Further reading

Recommended

In addition to this list of essential driving publications, please also visit our document library at:

www.mydriving.co.uk/document-library

i. **The Highway Code**. Available free online.

ii. **Know Your Traffic Signs**. Available free online.

iii. **Casualty Report** (Annual Government Statistics for road casualties). Available free online.

iv. **The Driving Instructor's Handbook, John Miller**. Purchase online or from a bookshop.

v. **Driving: The Essential Skills, HMSO.** Purchase online or from a bookshop.

vi. **Roadcraft, The Police Driver's Handbook (2021 Edition)**. Purchase online or from a bookshop.

vii. **Ultimate Driving Craft (DVD), Chris Gilbert**. www.driving4tomorrow.com -Purchase online

viii. **National standard for driving cars and light vans (Category B) – (DVSA Document)**. Available free online.

ix. **Driving Tests: Standard Operating Procedures (DVSA Document DT1)**. Available free online.

x. **Guidance of Driving Examiners conducting ADI tests and checks (DVSA Document ADI1)**. Available free online.

xi. **Coaching for Performance, John Whitmore.** Purchase online or from a bookshop.

xii. **Who's in the Driving Seat? Ged Wilmot & Claire Wilmot.** Purchase online or from a bookshop.

xiii. **An Insight to Drive. Kathy Higgins.** Purchase online or from a bookshop.

Internet Resources

Road Safety Knowledge Centre:www.roadsafetyknowledgecentre.org.uk

Road Safety GB: www.roadsafetygb.org.uk

Road Safety GB Academy: www.rsgbacademy.org.uk

Road Safety Campaigns: www.think.gov.uk

APPENDIX 8

GLOSSARY OF TERMS

Translating abbreviations

We live in a world of acronyms, and the driver trainer industry is no different. Below is a list of key terms which you'll need to know:

AA	Automobile Association
ABS	Anti-Lock Braking System
ADI	Approved Driving Instructor (Car)
ADINJC	ADI National Joint Council
ARRM	Association for Road Risk Management
BTEC	Business Technical & Education Council (Awarding Body: Edexcel)
CCL	Client-Centred learning
CPC	Certificate of Professional Competence
CPD	Continuing Professional Development
DCPC	Driver Certificate of Professional Competence
DIA	Driving Instructors Association
DVSA	Driver and Vehicle Standards Agency
ESP	Electronic Stability Programme
HGV	Heavy Goods Vehicle
IMTD	Institute of Master Tutors of Driving
IAM	Institute of Advanced Motorists
ITN	Identify Training Needs
LGV	Large Goods Vehicle
MiDAS	Minibus Driver Assessment Scheme
MSA	Motor Schools Association
NCAP	New Car Assessment Programme
NDORS	National Driver Offender Retraining Scheme
NPCC	National Police Chiefs Council
NSL	National Speed Limit
NVQ	National Vocational Qualification
ORDIT	Official Register of Driving Instructor Training
PDI	Potential Driving Instructor
PCV	Passenger Carrying Vehicle
PPE	Personal Protective Equipment
Q&A	"Question and Answer" Technique
RoSPA	Royal Society for the Prevention of Accidents
RPM	(Engine) Revs Per Minute
SOAP	Summary On A Page
USP	Unique Selling Point

APPENDIX 9

DRIVING TEST FORM

DL25

Driving Test Report

DL25A

0408 T

I declare that:
- the use of the test vehicle for the purposes of the test is fully covered by a valid policy of insurance which satisfies the requirements of the relevant legislation.
- I normally live/have lived in the UK for at least 185 days in the last 12 months (except taxi/private hire). See note 30.

✗ _____

Candidate

S ☐   D/C ☐

Application Ref. ☐☐☐ ☐☐☐ ☐☐☐ ☐☐☐

Date ☐☐ ☐☐ ☐☐   Time ☐☐☐☐   Dr./No. ☐☐☐☐☐☐

DTC Code / Authority ☐☐☐☐☐☐   Reg. No. ☐☐☐☐☐☐

Examiner

Staff / Ref. No. ☐☐☐☐☐☐

	Auto	Ext
Cat. Type ☐☐☐☐	☐	☐

1 ☐ 2 ☐ 3 ☐ 4 ☐ 5 ☐ 6 ☐ 7 ☐ 8 ☐ 9 ☐ 0 ☐ V ☐

Instructor Reg ☐☐☐☐☐☐

Instructor Cert ☐☐☐☐☐☐☐☐   Sup ☐   ADI ☐   Int ☐   Other ☐   C ☐

	Total S D		Total S D		Total S D
1a Eyesight	☐	**13 Move off** safety	☐☐☐	**23 Positioning** normal driving	☐☐☐
1b H/Code / Safety	☐☐☐	control	☐☐☐	lane discipline	☐☐☐
2 Controlled Stop	☐☐☐	**14 Use of mirrors- M/C rear obs** signalling	☐☐☐	**24 Pedestrian crossings**	☐☐☐
		change direction	☐☐☐	**25 Position / normal stops**	☐☐☐
3 Reverse / Left Reverse with trailer control	☐☐☐	change speed	☐☐☐	**26 Awareness / planning**	☐☐☐
observation	☐☐☐	**15 Signals** necessary	☐☐☐	**27 Ancillary controls**	☐☐☐
4 Reverse/ Right control	☐☐☐	correctly	☐☐☐	**28 Spare 1**	☐☐☐
observation	☐☐☐	timed	☐☐☐	**29 Spare 2**	☐☐☐
5 Reverse Park control	☐☐☐	**16 Clearance / obstructions**	☐☐☐	**30 Spare 3**	☐☐☐
R ☐ C ☐ obs.	☐☐☐	**17 Response to signs / signals** traffic signs	☐☐☐	**31 Spare 4**	☐☐☐
6 Turn in road control	☐☐☐	road markings	☐☐☐	**32 Spare 5**	☐☐☐
observation	☐☐☐	traffic lights	☐☐☐	**33 Wheelchair** Pass ☐ Fail ☐	
7 Vehicle checks	☐☐☐	traffic controllers	☐☐☐		
8 Forward park / control	☐☐☐	other road users	☐☐☐		
Taxi manoeuvre observation	☐☐☐	**18 Use of speed**	☐☐☐		

Pass ☐ Fail ☐ None ☐   Total Faults ☐☐   Route No. ☐☐

	Total S D		Total S D
9 Taxi wheelchair	☐	**19 Following distance**	☐☐☐
10 Uncouple / recouple	☐☐☐	**20 Progress** appropriate speed	☐☐☐
11 Precautions	☐☐☐	undue hesitation	☐☐☐
12 Control accelerator	☐☐☐	**21 Junctions** approach speed	☐☐☐
clutch	☐☐☐	observation	☐☐☐
gears	☐☐☐	turning right	☐☐☐
footbrake	☐☐☐	turning left	☐☐☐
parking brake / MC front brake	☐☐☐	cutting corners	☐☐☐
steering	☐☐☐	**22 Judgement** overtaking	☐☐☐
balance M/C	☐☐☐	meeting	☐☐☐
PCV door exercise	☐☐☐	crossing	☐☐☐

ETA V ☐ P ☐   D255 ☐

Survey A ☐ B ☐ C ☐ D ☐   E ☐ F ☐ G ☐ H ☐

Eco Safe driving   Control ☐   Planning ☐

Debrief ☐   Activity Code ☐

I acknowledge receipt of Pass Certificate Number: Licence rec'd
☐☐☐☐☐☐☐☐   Yes ✗

Wheelchair Cert. No: COA ✗
☐☐☐☐☐☐☐☐

No ✗

There has been no change to my health: see note 29 overleaf.

✗ _____

DVSA – An executive agency of the Department for Transport

Form Ref. DL25 D0018000-00

APPENDIX 10

STANDARDS CHECK FORM

SC1

Standards Check Form SC1

INFORMATION

Driver & Vehicle Standards Agency

Trainer Name		Location		Outcome
PRN		Date	/ /	
		Dual Controls	Yes No	
Valid Certificate	Yes No	Reg No.		
		Accompanied?	QA Trainer Other	

ASSESSMENT

	Competence
	0 1 2 3

Competence columns:
- 0 = No evidence
- 1 = Demonstrated in a few elements
- 2 = Demonstrated in most elements
- 3 = Demonstrated in all elements

Pupil: Beginner☐ Partly Trained☐ Trained☐ FLH New☐ FLH Experienced☐

Lesson theme: Junctions☐ Town & city driving☐ Interacting with other road users☐
Dual carriageway / faster moving roads☐ Defensive driving☐ Effective use of mirrors☐
Independent driving☐ Rural roads☐ Motorways☐ Eco-safe driving☐
Recap a manoeuvre☐ Commentary☐ Recap emergency stop☐ Other☐

LESSON PLANNING	0	1	2	3
Did the trainer identify the pupil's learning goals and needs?				
Was the agreed lesson structure appropriate for the pupil's experience and ability?				
Were the practice areas suitable?				
Was the lesson plan adapted, when appropriate, to help the pupil work towards their learning goals?				
Score for lesson planning				

RISK MANAGEMENT	0	1	2	3
Did the trainer ensure that the pupil fully understood how the responsibility for risk would be shared?				
Were directions and instructions given to the pupil clear and given in good time?				
Was the trainer aware of the surroundings and the pupil's actions?				
Was any verbal or physical intervention by the trainer timely and appropriate?				
Was sufficient feedback given to help the pupil understand any potential safety critical incidents?				
Score for risk management				

TEACHING & LEARNING STRATEGIES	0	1	2	3
Was the teaching style suited to the pupil's learning style and current ability?				
Was the pupil encouraged to analyse problems and take responsibility for their learning?				
Were opportunities and examples used to clarify learning outcomes?				
Was the technical information given comprehensive, appropriate and accurate?				
Was the pupil given appropriate and timely feedback during the session?				
Were the pupil's queries followed up and answered?				
Did the trainer maintain an appropriate non-discriminatory manner throughout the session?				
At the end of the session - was the pupil encouraged to reflect on their own performance?				
Score for teaching and learning strategies				
Overall score				

REVIEW

	YES	NO
Did the trainer score 7 or less on Risk Management? (A 'Yes' response to this question will result in an automatic Fail)		
At any point in the lesson, did the trainer behave in a way which put you, the pupil or any third party in immediate danger, so that you had to stop the lesson? (A 'Yes' response to this question will result in an automatic Fail)		
Was advice given to seek further development?		

Feedback offered to trainer

Examiner Name _____ Signature _____

C 1/2014

EPILOGUE

Graham Feest F Inst MTD, FARRM

Road Safety Consultant, Road Safety Advisor to the ADI National Joint Council, Chairman of the Institute of Master Tutors of Driving and Chairman of the National Road Safety Committee

The views expressed in this epilogue are those of the writer Graham Feest and do not necessarily represent the policy or views of any organisation for which he holds office.

Congratulations! You have now become a qualified Approved Driver Trainer, or have decided to set about joining the profession which brings with it a huge responsibility. There will be times when you are elated in what you have achieved, especially when celebrating with excited pupils whom you have helped to pass their test, but equally there will be times of despair, where those those you are training just don't seem to grasp the task at hand. Likewise, there might be times when you will question whether you have really done enough to ensure the long-term safety of your pupil, particularly when you hear that they have had a crash within weeks of graduating—as so many newly qualified drivers do. You are in a difficult position, as current thinking dictates that learning to drive is a series of mechanical exercises and manoeuvres, with a little knowledge about observation and anticipation all designed to pass a test.

There is, of course, a lot more to driving, but it is difficult to bring this into your teaching when most people will argue that knowing about wearing seatbelts, not using a mobile phone, keeping to the legal drink and drug limits, and obeying the speed limits is not really about the actual art of controlling the vehicle; which is what they come to learn from you. Introducing subject matter of this nature will be of little or no interest to many who have come to learn to drive, as they do not see this as part of the process. And yet, not only is it important, but the reasoning and science behind it is essential. As a driver trainer, this is an area that you need to know and understand.

Within the driving industry, we speak a lot about trying to change the mindset of those who want to learn to drive, but we do very little to develop a culture which would support such a move. The old adage that "what gets tested will get trained" is as true in this area as it is with any academic subject. We know from our school days that we just did not want to learn the things which were unlikely to come up in the examination, and teachers would spend hours researching old examination papers to access the frequency and likelihood of certain questions appearing in a particular year to give a steer of what should be learned.

So, as a new ADI, you need to equip yourself with all the background knowledge and understanding you can about driving, and what it means to be a safe driver **for life** across the theory, legal and practical elements of the task. Keeping your knowledge up to date is essential, and involving yourself in good quality support and CPD via trade and local associations is paramount to achieving this, along with the relationships you can build with other trainers who can help and support you when things are not going so well.

It is always helpful to have another trainer to whom you can lean on for guidance and support, and perhaps from time to time ask for help with a pupil who is just not grasping something from your approach. Or, if going down the route of undertaking a "mock test", what better way to do it than exposing your pupil to an unknown person? After all, that is what will happen in the real test situation.

Remember that as a driver trainer, people will regard you as an "expert" in a field much wider than just teaching people to drive, and the public expectation will be considerable. So, don't be surprised if you get a knock on the door because someone is having difficulty in fitting a child seat into their car; someone's got a puncture and can't undo their wheel nuts or change the wheel, or because their car won't start. There is a whole litany of issues regarding cars, for which people will now consider you the de-facto "guru".

Finally, take whatever opportunities you can to influence the attitudes of your pupils. By the time you have concluded their training, they will possess the skills to drive; but that does not make them a driver. During your lessons, they ought to have learned something about their responsibilities to other road users, and have learned something from you about the importance and value of always wearing a seatbelt and ensuring that their passengers do likewise; that alcohol and drugs do not mix with the driving task; that using a mobile phone for any purpose whilst driving whether hand-held or in a cradle is a dangerous practice, and that the speed limit is there for a reason—it is not a target which must be attained at all times. We refer to these as "the fatal four", as more lives are needlessly lost by these practices than by any other means. As an instructor, you should ensure that you have studied the information and got all your facts together about these issues, so you are prepared to answer questions—but whatever you do don't turn it into a lecture sat by the side of the road, as you will achieve nothing.

So now, let's take a look at a few other arguments about being a driver trainer. As you gain experience and share with others, you will become part of the debate about a variety of issues. Therefore it's vital for you to stay informed.

Is being a driver trainer a good career?

Think carefully before making the final decision to enter the driver training profession. It is important that you have an aptitude for teaching, and understand that techniques and approaches to giving instruction change over time as new and better methods develop. Consider carefully how many lessons you can do effectively in a day/week, and pace yourself accordingly. It is important to build a good relationship with your pupil, and where appropriate their parents too. This might mean having slightly fewer pupils per day, but your business will ultimately thrive if you build a good sustainable reputation, which in turn allows you to charge a realistic price for your services.

Once you have established yourself, then you can manage your workload in such a way as to get the flexibility to fit in other things, such as hobbies. At the end of the day, you will get as much elation as your pupil does when they successfully come to the end of their time with you.

How do you see the ADI Register changing?

Once qualified, you will be added to the Register of Approved Driving Instructors (ADI). This gives you the authority to charge for teaching someone to drive. Currently, that register sits with the government agency which is responsible for the conduct and standards of instructors, and also the ADI Register. In order to maintain your registration, you must conduct yourself in a fit and proper manner; the registrar will react swiftly to any complaints which are made, any of which could affect your registration and therefore your authority to continue practising.

For a long time now, there have been suggestions that the administration and approval process could be outsourced to a private company, in the same way that the theory and hazard perception test are currently. The practical driving test is also not excluded from this thought process, and from time to time the subject is re-visited. Whilst at some point this might become a reality, one would expect the standards required still to be set by the government or its agency.

Should qualified ADIs stay on the register for life, but be subject to periodic checks to be allowed to teach?

In order to maintain standards, you will have to undertake a periodic standards check. After qualifying, the check will happen fairly quickly. The life of your ADI Licence lasts for four years, and you can expect to be contacted at least once in that period for a standards check. You are legally obligated to make yourself available for that purpose, or your registration will be revoked, and you will then not be able to continue to give instruction. You also need to be aware that your test results are monitored. If said monitoring throws up anything of a continuous nature in terms of faults or a high number of failures, you might well be contacted for an additional standards check.

There is a view that either you are good enough to continue or you are not, but the current regime grades you an A, B, or at worst a failure. Many people believe that the grade system should not be for public consumption, but just used internally and monitored accordingly. I would tend to agree that this should be the case.

Providing you continue to maintain your standards, then you can continue to teach people to drive—there is no cut-off age where you need to forcibly retire. However, one would hope that you will realise when the time is right for you to surrender your licence.

Modernising of driver training. How much of this has been achieved?

No doubt, in the near future there will be changes in regard to what needs to be learned by new drivers, in order to keep up with the way in which the road network is developing. In recent times we have seen the introduction of independent driving, where the pupil is just told to follow the sat nav or a series of signs to a destination. The introduction of independent driving has proved very popular. It has answered one of the problems which used to arise, when a person who had just passed their test went out on their own. Here, they not only had to think about what they had learned in terms of manoeuvring, but they also had to think about navigating (where the trainer had always given verbal directions). However, there are concerns about how little time is spent training people to drive in the dark. This not only accounts for a number of crashes, but also is the time when young newly qualified people actually drive. We also fail to spend enough time with our learners on rural roads, where many newly qualified drivers are involved in single vehicle crashes. Drivers only learn to drive with a trainer sat in the front seat next to them, and do not experience people in the rear or how to cope and manage conversations unrelated to driving whilst undertaking the task. These are areas in which I can see some development in the future; and this development is long overdue. It could well mean that trainers will have to manage their time in a different way, in order to provide the proper experience for their pupils.

Should there be mandatory Continuing Professional Development (CPD) for ADIs?

There is no doubt in my mind that CPD for driver trainers should be of a compulsory nature, bringing driving in line with others who are trained to teach. If you wish to be regarded as a professional within your chosen career, it is essential to take time out to maintain your knowledge and standards, as well as improving yourself. CPD is not something which will cost you a lot of money, and many of the driver training associations provide CPD free of charge or on a cost recovery basis. Attempts by the government to introduce it back in the nineties/early 2000s (at the time of recession) failed, as they did not wish to burden business with any more regulatory processes.

CPD can take many forms, both on an individual basis—setting aside time to read up on relevant subject matter—on a group basis by attending specific subject-based sessions organised by trade associations and others, or by attending regular meetings to listen to speakers and discuss topical issues. Equally, CPD could take the form of signing up for a formal teaching qualification or business management course.

Does anyone use the National Standard for Driver and Rider Training?

As a driver trainer, you should be very familiar with the National Standard for Driver and Rider Training. It is a very clear and concise (but not exhaustive) minimum starting point, and clearly sets out what you need to achieve at a basic level with your pupils. You can always add more, but remember that when learning there is only so much that a person can absorb at a time. This is why many feel that reaching this standard as published should, and is, only a starting point. The same people believe that this should be followed by some formal process or other, to ensure that drivers are consistently raising their standards. However, to date, we have never mandated for this in the industry.

Should ADIs be allowed to sign off the reversing manoeuvres, freeing up more time for forward driving?

The question about who should sign off competency with regard to reversing and other manoeuvres is a long, ongoing debate. The first thing to say is that there are listed manoeuvres which a pupil might be asked to perform on their practical test, and generally only one or two will be selected. But, in terms of teaching your pupil, there are others which should not be ignored—such as turning the car round to face the opposite direction, which has recently been removed from the test list.

In order to guarantee that everything is taught to a competent level, it is my view that an independent person should be responsible for assessing any manoeuvres or for that matter any part of the test. Testing is pretty much always carried out by an independent person in most areas of life, and certainly not the person who has done the training.

Should the current "trainee driving instructor licence" scheme be replaced with a full supervision process?

I personally am somewhat critical of the way in which people can enter the driver training profession, and the manner in which they are taught their craft.

It is a fact that anyone can sign up to become a driver trainer ,and all they require is a driving licence and a clean DBS check certificate. There is no further screening as to whether or not you may have the temperament or ability to enter the profession, and many question whether that is the right approach. Ultimately, the instructor is undertaking the work of a teacher; we would not accept the same methodology used to train and appoint our teachers as we do driver trainers. So, why are we accepting lower standards for entry?

A driver trainer needs to know their craft, and for the most part they do. If they are deficient in that area, they get weeded out fairly early in the process, although it is known that many do in fact avail themselves of some refresher training prior to taking part two of the ADI test—which is a test of one's ability to drive to a high standard. Equally, they need to have knowledge of the highway code and motoring matters. You might say in teacher training terms that would be about passing your "A-levels" before going off to teacher training college.

It is at this point that they start to learn how to teach, and the various methods which can be employed in doing so. Here we need to remember something: it does not follow that just because you can do something well, you can teach someone else to do likewise. You would not expect your child to be taught by a teacher in school who was not qualified to do so, and yet we don't apply the same kind of standard when it comes to driver trainers. In my view, all driver trainers should have attained some qualification in terms of teaching, as well as being able to instruct in the car. We find many would-be instructors having to take their part three examinations on more than one occasion, and this is the element which is to do with the teaching.

Fortunately, there are many competent driver trainers who specialise in helping people to achieve their part three examination via training and mentoring, in a way that's similar to the teacher in the classroom. This part of the process works well, but you should also choose your mentor carefully. Make enquiries to ensure that if you are wishing to become an instructor, you go to the best person. Find someone who suits you as a person and your personality, and do not be afraid of them constantly sitting in the car when you are conducting a lesson—as that is what should happen until you are qualified.

Do you feel that the issue of safeguarding has been recognised sufficiently in the ADI industry?

I am confident in saying that the issue of safeguarding has been well-recognised by the industry, but whether it has been fully understood by the individuals working within it is another question. More work needs to be done to fully explain to people how to conduct themselves when dealing with other people. What was acceptable in terms of the spoken word and physical actions in the past, is certainly different nowadays, and many trainers who have been around for a long time have had great difficulty with areas such as adjusting their vocabulary, harmless banter, and innocent touching to guide a pupil, without it giving rise to complaint.

The ADI Registrar will act very positively if they receive complaints from any member of the public in this area, and we all have to be very much on a guard. Remember, you yourself might not mind a word or two here and there, or a tap of support on the back, but others—particularly those whom you don't know very well—might. Don't fall into the familiarity trap. Just because you've been working with a pupil for some weeks, and feel like you know them well enough to have a joke, it doesn't mean you can let your guard down. Be careful about what you say and how you behave.

Has allowing learners to drive to motorways with an ADI been a success?

This rather depends on how one measures success. Clearly, there is no problem with allowing learners onto motorways under such supervision where it is practical to do so, and when the time is right. Motorways have changed significantly in how they operate, and this means that there is a lot more to learn about this type of road than in the past. Having the opportunity to learn about this with a driver trainer is ideal. Regretfully, a vast number of learner drivers go nowhere near a motorway during their lessons, so do not get this added experience. In addition, some driver trainers are reluctant or not bothered about using the motorway, since it does not form part of the test.

The question for the future is when and whether we will allow learner drivers to use motorways when being supervised by a qualified driver (non-ADI) for practice purposes, and there are certainly calls for that to be allowed to happen.

Should a statutory "record of achievement" be introduced as part of the learning to drive process?

It is a basic concept of education and training that a record of progress and achievement should be recorded and available, and could be presented to the examiner at the time of the test—demonstrating that instruction has taken place and that the pupil has demonstrated competence. In the driving industry, there is a lot of criticism over driver trainers putting people in for the test before they are ready. So, a record of achievement would go some way to demonstrating that they have at least covered all the areas required. We need to remember that the test itself is a contract between the testing authority and the pupil, and some pupils go against the advice of the trainer and book a test before they are ready or have achieved all that they should in their training. So, a record of achievement could really help here too.

Should the "Pass-Plus" scheme be scrapped or re-vamped. If the latter, how could it be made more effective?

This process, in its current form, is totally discredited. Many driver trainers claim that what is included in Pass-Plus is taught anyway during regular lessons, and that now learners are allowed on motorways (which used to be the missing element) there is little need for Pass-Plus in its present form.

In my view, if we are wishing to place restrictions onto newly qualified drivers—such as driving at night/in the dark, carrying x number of passengers at a reduced drink-drive limit, and from driving in certain areas where high risks and crashes have been identified (such as rural roads) then Pass-Plus might have some value, as we can maintain said restrictions until said drivers have undertaken specific training in these areas. It is, however, a course which I would encourage driver trainers to take part in. I feel that at some point in the future, we could embark on a further training programme (be it on a statutory or voluntary basis) which would enhance driving skills. Therefore, it would be a shame to throw Pass-Plus out altogether.

Should graduated driving be introduced? If so, what format should it take?

I have always had a bit of a problem with what people talk about in terms of "graduated licence or driving." All of the ideas put forward have been about restricting drivers from doing things for a short period, and then—as if by magic—without any intervention of any kind, after x number of months those restrictions just get removed. I personally feel that we need a new focus, and we need to be clear about what we want, whilst ensuring that whatever might be put into place is sustainable.

Do ADIs prepare learners enough for driving on rural national speed limit roads, where so many casualties occur?

The simple answer to this question is NO, to which you might ask, 'Well, why not?' Again, it's all about the test, and that is where we have the whole process wrong. Irrespective of what people might say, learners **are** taught to pass a test. That test does not take place on true rural roads, so why would a trainer spend much of their time in that environment?

Is the driving test fit for purpose? If not, what changes would you make?

I do not like the current manner in which we conduct the driving test, as it is based on a fault-finding exercise—which is contrary to education principles. In my mind it is far too black and white, and does not really assess the overall performance of the learner. Having said that, you need to replace it with an alternative method, which is seen to be fair. That's what is proving so difficult, and therefore I believe we simply have to grin and bear the current outdated approach.

Against that comment, however, the current British driving test is held up around the world as being one of the best— and many people would agree with our approach to doing things, and with the view that only those who can demonstrate good competence should be allowed to drive on the road unsupervised.

Has the use of in-vehicle monitoring telematics been a success?

There is no doubt that telematics has been a success in driving down the number of newly qualified drivers who are involved in fatal and serious crashes, and the insurance companies will bear testament to that in terms of their claims experience.

Many newly qualified and young drivers cannot get insurance, or pay very heavily for refusing to accept the use of telematic technology in their vehicle. Telematics also helps to control when the car is driven, as the insurance package will cost more for those who drive at night rather than in daylight hours.

Will we soon only be teaching in automatic electric vehicles?

It now makes total sense for driver trainers to invest in electric cars. Assuming we continue on the current trend, geared cars will soon be a thing of the past, and by 2030 I imagine that almost all cars will be automatic, electric vehicles. Likewise, we know that more people now learning in cars that have automatic transmission. In the shorter term, we will need to explore our licencing regulations, making provisions for those who pass their test in an automatic transmission vehicle to be able to drive a geared car, perhaps by means of a conversion course.

Will electric vehicles lead to safer roads?

There is no evidence to say that electric vehicles will mean fewer crashes, and therefore safer roads. Ultimately, the control of such vehicles will still be in the hands of a human, and by our very nature people make mistakes.

Finally, if you were Transport Minister for a day, what changes would you bring in?

Earlier in this chapter, I made the point that becoming a driving instructor means people's expectations of you will change. At times, this can be difficult, especially when someone asks you a question that you don't (and shouldn't necessarily) know the answer to. For example, being a driving instructor doesn't make you a mechanic, so you can't always tell people why their car won't start! This, particular question, however, is something I am frequently asked as a final question during panels. So, I have rehearsed my response many times over:

- Have a more stringent and appropriate screening process for those seeking to enter the profession, with a pre-requisite of some form of teaching and training certificate such as PTILLS or equivalent.

- Introduce mandatory CPD for the driver training profession, of at least one day per year in a face-to-face environment.

- Restructure the Register of Driving Instructors, to include all those who provide training and not just those who teach drivers to pass their initial driving test.

On the basis of "what gets tested, gets taught" I would:

- Mandate that a percentage of the test would take place in the dark/ night.

- Make the test longer, even if that means having fewer tests each day, so that a better assessment could be made of people driving on rural, derestricted roads.

- Mandate that all people wishing to learn to drive must take professional lessons from a qualified trainer.

In conclusion, I wish you well in your career as a driver trainer.

Graham Feest
January 2023

Printed in Great Britain
by Amazon

24095092R00143